MUSIC for the MODERN DANCE

BROWN

PHYSICAL EDUCATION SERIES

Edited by AILEENE LOCKHART,
University of Southern California, Los Angeles, Calif.

MUSIC
FOR THE
MODERN DANCE

PIA GILBERT

Associate Supervisor of Physical Education
and Resident Composer for Dance
University of California, Los Angeles

and

AILEENE LOCKHART

Professor of Physical Education and Education
University of Southern California, Los Angeles

Music by
Pia Gilbert

Illustrations by
Carol and Robert Scothorn

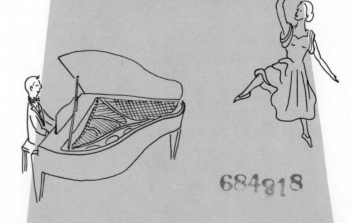

WM. C. BROWN COMPANY PUBLISHERS
135 SOUTH LOCUST STREET ● DUBUQUE, IOWA

Library of Congress Catalog Card Number: 60-53257

Copyright 1961
by
Pia Gilbert
and
Aileene Lockhart

Manufactured by
WM. C. BROWN CO. INC., Dubuque, Iowa
Printed in U. S. A.

To the memory of our fathers

Richard Wertheimer
Thomas Ellis Lockhart

TABLE OF CONTENTS

A LETTER TO THE READER ix

1. INTRODUCTION 1

2. THE ELEMENTS OF MUSIC FOR DANCE 3

   Rhythm 3
   Melody 4
   Harmony 4
   Dynamics 4
   Tempo 4
   Tone Color 4
   Form 4
   Good Form 7
   Review 7

3. PRINCIPLES OF ACCOMPANIMENT 8

   Accompaniment for Technical Work 8
   Accompaniment for Movement Fundamentals 13
   Accompaniment for Beginning Improvisation 13
   Observer-Assistants to the Accompanist 14

4. PERCUSSION INSTRUMENTS 15

   The Playing of Instruments 15
   The Care of Percussion Instruments 15
   The Construction of Percussion Instruments 16
   The Piano as a Percussion Instrument 18

5. MUSICAL NOTATION 22

   Rhythmic Symbols 23
   Melodic Symbols 24

6. TEACHER-ACCOMPANIST RELATIONSHIPS 28

   What To Look For in a Dance Accompanist 28
   Current Practices Relative to the Accompanist 31

7. CHOREOGRAPHER AND COMPOSER **33**

8. MUSIC FOR THE DANCE PERFORMANCE **36**

Balance and Theatrics 36
Choice of Music 36
Recorded Versus "Live" Music 37
Music as a Stimulus for Choreographic Effort 38
Placement of the Musicians 38

9. ACCOMPANIMENT FOR FOLK DANCE **40**

The Folk Dance Accompanist 40
Development of Basic Folk Dance Steps 41

10. A BRIEF HISTORY OF MUSIC FOR THE DANCE **44**

Monodic Music 45
Polyphonic Music 45
The Renaissance 45
The Baroque Period 46
The Classical Period 46
The Romantic Period 47
The Twentieth Century 47
Sequential Events in Music-Dance History 48

11. MODERN MUSIC **56**

Development of the Modern Style 56
Composers of the Twentieth Century 57

12. CONTEMPORARY COMPOSERS FOR DANCE **59**

Composers for Dance 59
Dance-Accompanist Composers 61

13. RESOURCES **63**

Piano Works 63
Recordings 65
Selected References 70

14. DANCE ACCOMPANIMENT **73**

Dance Techniques 73
Dance Composition 91
Folk Dance Suite 103
Pre-Classic Suite 112

A LETTER TO THE READER

The main *raison d'être* for our book is the clarification and disentanglement of an area of great concern to choreographers, accompanists, teachers, performers, and students of the dance, viz.—THE MUSIC! *Where* to find it, *what* to do with it, *how* to cope with it. We are vitally interested in finding ways and means of bringing about an organic interaction between the two media of dance and music, whether the musical composition existed before the birth of the dance idea or was created specifically with it in mind.

We have tried to divide the contents of this book in as logical and orderly a manner as possible; it, therefore, contains the usual chapters, headings, and subheadings. But we implore you to *read the book as a total work first,* and refer to individual topics later. We have not, in other words, repeated information; we are counting on knowledge and concepts gathered along the way.

You will discover by the tone and the general genre of the book that we have set down a minimum of hard and fast rules. Anything as flexible, fleeting, and individual as music and dance should not and cannot ever be constrained with strict laws. Certain guidelines, however, have been set up; these should be taken to heart and in some instances, followed to the letter. It is our earnest hope that the general and specific knowledges and skills which you may receive, ultimately will free rather than restrain you, and will lead to experimentation which will be followed by real creativity within the areas to which the book has exposed you.

We have enjoyed writing this volume. It was challenging and helpful to us to have been forced to put into words some of that which we do not believe has been expressed previously on the written page, and which was, as a consequence, only partially available to the uninitiated.

Before we close we should like to acknowledge our indebtedness and express sincere appreciation to our friends, our teachers, our colleagues, and our students, all of whom have through the years contributed interest, advice, tutelage, and inspiration.

PIA GILBERT and AILEENE LOCKHART

MUSIC

FOR THE

MODERN DANCE

Chapter 1

Music and dance are sister arts and have all their most basic elements in common. They both need rhythm, tempo, balance, dynamics, stress, melody, harmony, tone color, space, and form in order to create their visual and audible images separately and together. It is therefore possible for them to be coexisting within the same time element. It is also possible for them to live apart; however the perceiver of one or the other usually furnishes what is unseen or unheard through his individual inner imagery.

What makes us dance? What compels us to make music? Which came first and therefore conditioned the second? These have always been fascinating questions for the person who is interested in history, aesthetics, and philosophy. Many excellent books deal directly or indirectly with this subject. In our estimation, these explorations deal in essence with the presumed order and conditions of the development of ORGANIZED MOVEMENT (dance) and its related art, ORGANIZED SOUND (music).

Since music was from its very onset, as far as is known, officially designed as a stimulus for dance—from its primitive pulsating beginnings through the fairly elaborate period of the preclassic dance and then the ornateness of the classic ballets—its intimate association with visual movement cannot be denied. Regardless of the composer's intent, he usually depends, consciously or not, upon the audience's sense of "inner dance" for the success of his work. The support of movement, seen or imagined, is a basic heritage of music.

Through the years, music has somehow grown to be the more seemingly independent of the two arts. A musical concert is no longer an historic event, and by turning a little knob we can have a profusion of sound in the house, in the car, anywhere in fact, at any time. Music has become wonderfully accessible to everyone, this in contrast to the past when only the financially elite could afford either to go to concerts or to hire musicians and composers for their courts and salons. (This, of course, excludes the many "house musicians" who have always existed, people who played for their own pleasure and enjoyment). Our present ability to communicate anything with ease and speed via the airwaves, plus the wonderfully immense treasure of notated material which is now available to the musician have resulted in the obvious with regard to the former traditional dance-music relationship: music at present is more accessible, independent, and understood than dance.

The two arts are naturally still as basically related as ever and their complementary functions are perceived by the audience as before, but less and less has this become a conscious experience. Whereas the dance is still very much aware of the sounds that accompany it or that it accompanies, whichever the case may be, music is now more often than not unconcerned about movement except when it specifically sets out to support it. One can, in fact, hear many a composer or musician say of dancers or choreographers who are making artistic demands on them, "We can get along quite well without them, but they would certainly be lost without us." This situation is quite problematic and has resulted in some serious misunderstandings and deplorably poor working relationships between dancers and musicians. The problem is discussed more fully in a later chapter; suffice it to say for the moment that the dance-music area is in need of a renaissance of mutual and sympathetic endeavors.

A good deal of educating needs to be done. Musicians need to be trained in the surprisingly stimulating art of dance accompaniment and composition for choreography. This could and should become a rich and fertile professional field worthy of a life's devotion instead of a sideline. Dancers, on the other hand, need to be initiated into the fundamentals of music analysis, form and composition, so that they can work intelligently with a professional musical partner. When these needs have become accomplished, then we can look forward to a wholly new and a more natural kind of artistic and pedagogical balance both in the concert hall and in the dance studio.

The contents of this book, therefore, are directed toward an understanding of the relationships between dance and music, the teacher and accompanist, and the composer and choreographer. Both the professional musician and dancer will find much that they already know within their own medium in these pages, but it is hoped that for each, a study of this material may result in deepened and widened appreciation, knowledge, and understanding of the complementary art form. And for present students of both dance and music, it is hoped that the contents of these pages may help to circumvent future misunderstandings between the two fields and thereby promote the fertile, exciting relationship between the two which would so enhance each.

Chapter 2

THE ELEMENTS OF MUSIC FOR DANCE

When we talk about dance accompaniment, we are referring to an audible score by means of which dance movement may be sustained, contrasted, and supported. It is of paramount importance to bring out by means of organized sound or musical emphasis exactly what it is about the movement that needs to be supported accoustically. An effort is made, therefore, to attain a sensitive balance between that which is seen and that which is heard. Effective dance accompaniment, strictly speaking, is more supplement or complement to the movement than balance; its function is to sustain, to underlie, and at the same time to point up and highlight.

There are endless varieties of dance situations and as many opportunities for accompaniment variations, especially in the area of modern dance. In the classroom there is need for accompaniment for warm-ups, technique-sequences, and compositional ventures. There are dance concerts which call for newly composed scores and/or the selection of suitable works. There are theater situations which involve complex choreographies which need accompaniment to enhance or dramatically complete the plot. Music must be found for all of these.

Music for dance can be fashioned to the choreography, or a prewritten composition may act as a springboard for dance composition. In the latter case, the resulting dance would be a comment, or, very strictly speaking, an accompaniment to the music. In any event, there should be a fusion of movement and sound, one supporting and stimulating the other, now the music taking over, now the movement.

It must be remembered that the normal human eye usually is a more alert organ than the ear. It has been trained since infancy constantly to be on guard to stop us from bumping into things or into each other, to show us where we are, and to make us alert to the shapes, sizes, and the kinds of movement around us. It therefore takes a good bit of concentra-

tion, even on the part of the seasoned musical concert goer, to concentrate on the sound *only,* and not to be visually carried away by the elegant movements of the conductor, the acrobatics of the pianist, or the ballistics of the percussionists. At a dance concert, the music is only an integral part of the whole proceedings, and certainly the audience cannot very well be asked to close its eyes, as it often does at the usual musical concert, in order to concentrate.

It is not always easy for composers to devote their efforts to the modern dance. For one reason, their scores for dance should not be really self-sufficient, since ideally they should be fused with the movement, and, for another, the scores, because of this, cannot be given the complete attention that they would receive ordinarily. Only the composer who loves and understands both dance and music can find reward and gratification in such efforts.

Since it will be necessary to refer to them throughout the following pages, it might be beneficial to review briefly the well known *ingredients of music,* most of which have exact parallels in dance though occasionally under different synonyms. The components of music are rhythm, melody, harmony, dynamics, tempo, tone color, and form. These elements are very closely interrelated but are in essence entirely separate entities.

RHYTHM

Rhythm is the foundation and the most essential element of any art form. Its essence is *pulsations,* and therefore movement, the basis of life itself. It is a pattern of accents, visual or audible, repetitive or unpredictable in time. In music, these accents are spaced above a flow of continuous and driving pulses or beats which in the dance language constitutes the "underlying beat." Time measured into metric units, or MEASURES, is the result of steadily or less steadily recurring accents at the beginning of each unit. The measures contain a fixed number of beats, such as

2 or 4 or 5 or 6, and each beat receives its value in time fractions. Thus ¾ rhythm means that there are three beats per measure, and that each beat is worth a quarter note in time.

MELODY

Melody is *any* series of *consecutive* tones; it is the forward progression of tones—that is really all melody is. However, we are conditioned to thinking of melodies as being a succession of tones based on various modal systems, such, for example, as our Western eight tone major and minor scales, or some Eastern five tone or pentatonic scales.

HARMONY

Harmony is a series of *simultaneous* tones. It consists of coexisting combinations which usually are designed to support and anchor strategic melody tones. If the resulting sounds are in agreement, giving a reposed or unstrained effect, the chord is said to be *consonant*. On the other hand if there is a feeling of discord or lack of resolution, the chord is termed *dissonant*. The interplay between these two qualities is the basis of musical harmony. Harmony gives to music that feeling which depth and space give to painting.

DYNAMICS

The *interplay* between the quality and quantity of energy expended is known as dynamics. It is the HOW (percussive or sustained), the HOW MUCH (loud, soft), and the WHEN (tempo, rhythm) of things happening within the presentation, and its main contributions lie in the areas of *contrast* and *balance*.

The universal language of musical notation is Italian, and therefore the indications for the dynamics are always recorded in that tongue. Thus:

Quality of energy expended:
STACCATO ....Percussive

LEGATO ....Sustained

PORTAMENTO ....Detached
        (This is somewhere
        b e t w e e n staccato
        and legato.)

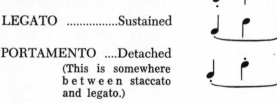

Quantity of energy expended:
PIANO ....Soft ---p
PIANISSIMO ....Very Soft ---pp
MEZZO PIANO ....Medium Soft ---mp
FORTE ....Loud ---f
FORTISSIMO ....Very Loud ---ff to fffff
MEZZO FORTE ....Medium Loud

An increase in volume is designated by this sign: and is labeled a CRESCENDO.

A decrease in volume is designated by this sign: and is labeled DECRESCENDO or DIMINUENDO.

TEMPO

Tempo refers to the speed at which the composition is being performed, or the rate at which the pulsations follow one another. The tempo may be slow or fast, or any intermediate point between the two. (*Tempo and Rhythm are not interchangeable terms* at any time. They influence each other occasionally, but they have completely separate identities. Nothing ever happens in a ¾ Tempo, for instance, only in a ¾ Rhythm.)

Again, as was explained under the section on dynamics, Italian is used to make the reading of musical directions more common throughout the world. Some examples:

ANDANTE ....In a walking tempo
MODERATO ....Moderately fast or slow
LENTO ....Slow
ADAGIO ....Slow with a singing quality
LARGO ....Slow with a heavy quality
VIVACE ....Lively
ALLEGRO ....Lively, fast, usually cheerful, "dancey"
PRESTO ....Very fast
An increase in Tempo is called acceleration. (ACCELERANDO)
A decrease in Tempo is labeled retardation. (RITARDANTO)

TONE COLOR

Various instruments and voices produce unique and characteristic *timbre* or tonal *shadings*. The composer has a musical tone palette at his disposal, similar to the color assortment available to the painter. The painter has his primary colors and with these can produce desired shadings and tones. Similarly the musical composer uses the four groups of instruments available to him: (1) the strings (violin, viola, violoncello, string bass), (2) the woodwinds (flute, oboe, clarinet, bassoon), (3) the brasses (trombone, tuba, trumpet, French horn), and (4) the percussion group (piano, cymbals, gongs, tympani, xylophone, drums). It makes an important tonal difference whether a tune or passage is played on the violin, the bassoon, by a small ensemble, on the piano, or whether it is sung by a soprano, a baritone, or a mixed chorus, or whether it is provided with orchestral background.

FORM

Form is the *plan*, the structure, the organization of parts, or the framework of a composition. It is sometimes said that "form is to music what plot is to a story; it is the order in which things happen." It seems to us that this analogy is not a precise one, however; a "plot" is concerned with the development of an idea whereas "form" is more specifically the particular design of its presentation. At any rate it is clear that the two should be intimately related. Actually the form of any art should evolve from its purpose and its content.

Musical form is always determined by the character of the main THEME. A theme is a short musical (or in dance, movement) idea which may be used as a subject for development and variation. The theme constitutes the thread which holds the piece together into a meaningful and coherent whole. Usually the main theme is introduced at the beginning, and after one or more new themes have been introduced, it recurs in toto or in variation form.

Subdivisions within the overall form are designated as PARTS, (Part A, Part B, etc.). These parts contain the *development* of the main theme and the secondary or counter themes via PHRASES or musical sentences. Just as the author develops a plot through related sentences which are built into paragraphs and subsequently into chapters and so on, the musician communicates his idea via phrases which are developed into parts, which expand the main theme within the overall form of the composition.

A careful examination of the methods that are used by composers in building satisfying forms and in employing economical means of developing strong contrapuntal music should be of great value to the dancer. A brief survey of the most commonly used compositional forms in music follows. Each has its counterpart in dance composition.

AB or TWO PART FORM

It is customary to represent different themes by letters A, B, C and so on. Each letter represents one idea. In a two part, or *binary form,* two complementary subjects are introduced. The composition begins with A, the presentation of one theme. Then B, a contrasting or associated element, is brought in. The two parts balance each other.

ABA or THREE PART FORM

The ABA, or *ternary form,* is a favorite in every type of music and dance, past and present. First the theme A is introduced and developed; a new theme B, which is related to A either by complementing it or contrasting it, is presented. This is followed by a return of the principal theme, A, which reappears either in intact or in variation form and brings the composition to a very satisfying completion.

RONDO or RONDEAU

The Rondo was a favorite among the classic and early romantic composers because of its lively and graceful flavor. A composition still *must* have this "vivace" air as well as the prescribed form to be named *Rondo.* Any other study using the ABACA form, but

which does not have the Rondo flavor, is simply designated as a SEQUENTIAL FORM.

The Rondo form was developed from a lively "round dance," where the group danced a fixed pattern in a circle; this was followed by soloists' improvisations in the center. Others have ascribed the name simply to the fact that the music comes round to the main theme again and again. At any rate, the rondo thus demands a return to the leading theme after distinct digressions.

The sequential pattern, and also the levity of spirit of the dance are still in evidence in our present musical Rondo. The main pattern is that of an inevitable return to theme A after other themes have been introduced. The main motif is repeated often. Occasionally it may reappear only as a fragment, while at other times the theme is highly embellished, or interestingly varied. But its return is assured.

A typical Rondo might look like this: *A, B, A, C, B1* (Variation on B), *A1, C, A2, transition, A3, transition, C2, Cadenza* (virtuoso passage), and a final variation on A. TRANSITIONS, or "bridges," help themes flow into each other easily and interestingly. Sometimes a CODA, or "tail ending" is tacked on to the final A; this closing section consists of a strong restatement or resolving conclusion.

Briefly then, a rondo is a lively piece of music, with a graceful, eighteenth century air, which follows a sequential pattern, and includes a frequent return to its main theme.

THEME AND VARIATIONS (A, A1, A2, A3, A4 . . .)

This is essentially a *stringing together* of the same theme which has been changed or altered melodically, harmonically, rhythmically, or dynamically. (Add direction and level changes for dance!) Each variation emphasizes an important manipulation of the thematic elements.

The variations may be separate entities with a pause before the presentation of the following one, or they may flow one into another without any break.

SUITE

The Suite is *a collection of pieces* loosely related and gathered together under one heading or descriptive title. The Suite was a favorite form prior to the development of the Sonata. Originally, Suites were written for the court dances, or "Preclassic Dances" as we like to refer to them, and they included lively dances where the feet left the ground (haute danses), and stately dances (basse danses). Both types originally were known as Branles. The dignified Pavane and the lively Galliard formed the original Suite, and they were later joined by the Sarabande, the Courrante, the Allemande, the Gigue, and still later by the Gavotte and Minuet (refer to *Pre-Classic Dance Forms* by Louis Horst). Composers still write dance suites, but even more often now they write suites which have a story or picture thread as their common denominator.

SONATA

The Sonata is a direct descendent from the Suite; this explains the leftover term MOVEMENT, which names its sections. It is (and has been for the past two centuries) a major musical work consisting of three or four movements, the first of which is the SONATA ALLEGRO, whose form is best described as a giant *A B A*. It is the kind of three-part form which we find very often in literature, namely the design of EXPOSITION, DEVELOPMENT, and RECAPITULATION.

The first movement of the Sonata (Sonata Allegro) is developed as follows: The *Exposition, A*, contains the presentation of the main themes, often three—the first one being a strongly dramatic or "masculine" theme (a), the second a contrastingly lyrical or "feminine" idea (b), and a last theme (c) which consists of a closing statement or comment.

The *Development*, section *B*, includes a free manipulation of the three themes which were introduced during the exposition, and may add new and more elaborate material to enhance the main character of the original thematic content.

The *Recapitulation, A*, brings back in essence that which was presented originally; however some modal, or key changes, and possibly some slight variations are made.

The second movement of the overall Sonata is usually a lyrical ANDANTE or an ADAGIO.

If the Sonata is made up of four movements, then the third movement is often a dance such as the *Minuet* or the dance-like *Scherzo*. The minuet, which takes its name from the word "menu" meaning small and mincing, is a ¾ dance form which became popular in the seventeenth century. The Scherzo, literally "joke" or "jest," is capricious by nature and is written in compact *A B A* form. The last movement of the Sonata is lively, fast, and often is a Rondo in form.

Sonatas written for more than two instruments are known as TRIOS, QUARTETTES, and so on. A Sonata written for full symphony orchestra is known as the SYMPHONY, and one written for a solo instrument with orchestral accompaniment goes under the title of a CONCERTO.

Some Contrapuntal Forms

The essence of counterpoint or POLYPHONY (more than one voice or melody) is the architectural manipulation of one or more melodies at the same time. As can be imagined, any contrapuntal music demands the almost undivided attention of the listener since part of its interest lies within the cleverness of its structure. Its appeal is almost scientific and mathematical. This does not rob contrapuntal music of emotional impact, however. In fact, the Bach preludes and fugues, for example, are very stirring pieces of art. The austerity of their form adds to the spirit and profound passion of the music. Most polyphonic music is rather short and concise, and includes no "wasted" measures or even unnecessary notes. Its architectural essence has great potential for dance choreography.

CANON

One of the most famous contrapuntal forms is the *Round* or *Canon*, which consists of a melody that contains the compatible harmonic ingredients which allow it to be played with and against itself. At strategic points within the melody, new beginnings of the same tune can be played or sung; this combination results in a satisfying harmonic structure.

It lies within the skill of the composer to devise melodies which have the potentiality of being independent and yet are interdependent enough to exist musically within the same piece at the same time. It is possible to have as many as four melodies (VOICES, as they are called) interwoven within the same piece, with at least two of them working simultaneously.

FUGUE

The most complicated but possibly also the most satisfying contrapuntal form is the *fugue*. It is in essence the exposition of three or four voices, which enter somewhere in the middle of the previous voice. Counterthemes (or countervoices) are introduced and an intermeshing of all this material occurs. This usually leads to an excited and exciting climax or STRETTO shortly before the end, and a recapitulation of the original theme.

The first theme, or SUBJECT, is of course the paramount material of the fugue and is heard practically throughout. It appears in various ranges of tone color, and is repeated by IMITATION; that is, it is played immediately following or during the presentation of its melody. Imitation, then, is actually that which also happens in a round or canon. Then there is the technique of INVERSION which is a device of practically turning the melody on its head; another contrapuntal technique is that of CANCRIZANS, (crab motion) in which the melody is played backward. All of these devices are used in the so-called contrapuntal forms.

GROUND BASS

Ground bass is an easiy recognizable kind of variation form. It is founded on a repeated figure in the bass (thus BASSO OSTINATO), and continues with this same pattern over and over. A presentation first is made of this sustained, uninterrupted theme; into this are woven contra developments and new thematic materials. The dance possibilities of the ground bass form are numerous.

Free Forms
PRELUDE

There are of course many other musical forms, especially in the realm of the so-called "free forms."

The *prelude* is an example; this form of composition originally was merely an improvisational effort played by the performer before the program per se got under way. The preludes were short, unpredictable in mood, and musical "curtain raisers" by function. Later on, any piece which was based mainly upon *one* theme or general quality-essence might be termed a Prelude. The term also is used loosely as the title for an introductory section (as, for example, to a suite or a fugue).

NOCTURNE

There are *nocturnes*, or "night pieces" which are lyrically melodic or dreamy in character. They often fall into an *A B A* pattern with *B* being a dramatic or passionate interruption, or a climax, within the reflective singing mood.

TONE POEM

There are the *tone poems* which fall within the general realm of PROGRAM MUSIC, a term which encompasses all music that sets out to arouse *specifically* planned, concrete imagery in the listener. Such works have descriptive titles and may follow a musically translated story line, a pictorial impression, or the like.

Composers usually title their works by the form that they have taken, or simply by a tempo indication. Music quickly can be made to suggest anything in the listener's mind other than that which he would ordinarily "see" while hearing the music. Unless the composer specifically designated a piece as program music, imagery should be left to the listener's inner eye. It is not entirely fair, therefore, to suggest that a piece of music represents rain or thunder, or wild horses, unless the composer expressly so titled his work.

ACCUMULATIVE FORM

Although it seems to make for a more satisfying formal structure to bring back the main theme *A* within a composition, there is no reason to force the return of *A* if the piece does not logically or emotionally warrant this restatement. The composition might therefore stop at *B* as it does in the two-part form, or it might simply add themes *C D E* and stop at *F*. In the latter case we have an example of an *accumulative form*.

GOOD FORM

There are endless variations on the so-called "set" forms. This is obviously necessary for if the descriptions of their organization were always adhered to explicitly, many dull compositions would otherwise undoubtedly result. The main guideline for *good form* in any art medium is not so much that of following a prescribed pattern to the letter but rather that of structuring a satisfying and complete whole. Good form results in a feeling of unity, of integrity, and of logic. Without it there can be no real shape or structure, and hence no real coherence.

REVIEW

For a quick "action review" of musical elements, let us take apart the folk song, "Swanee River."

1. *Melody:* Sing the melodic pattern, and try to concentrate on the rise and fall of the tones.
2. *Harmony:* Envision chords and intervals at the important melodic points.
3. *Rhythm:* (a) Sing the melody and clap the *underlying beat.*
   (b) Now clap the *rhythmic pattern.*
   (c) Find out where the primary accents occur. Since the primary accents seem to happen after every four underlying beats, we are in 4/4 time.
4. *Tone Color:* Imagine the piece played or sung by a children's chorus; a cello; a brass band; a banjo.
5. *Dynamics:* Listen for percussive and sustained sections, louder and softer passages.
6. *Form:* Designate the ends of phrases by punctuating with commas, periods, dashes, etc. "Swanee River" is an A B A form.

Chapter 3

PRINCIPLES OF ACCOMPANIMENT

There are numerous ways to support and enhance dance movement with accompanying sound. The most frequently and successfully applied techniques lie in the area of PARALLEL accompaniment and COMPLE-MENTARY accompaniment. These involve the principles of *relating* the accompaniment to the movement by clothing it with closely analogous, corresponding music, or *commenting* upon the movement by introducing contrast and variation.

Since dance involves a constant flux of natural stresses or accents, the rhythmic element is almost always paramount. All the ingredients of music play important accompanimental roles; however sometimes various elements are deliberately omitted or underplayed within a phrase or section, or indeed, within a complete work. It is not an infrequent occurrence, for example, to have a dance accompaniment score consist of a sparse rhythmic line executed on a woodblock or triangle, and it is also not out of the question to have dance accompanied by a full-bodied score which demands that it be played by an orchestra for melodic, harmonic, dynamic, and tone color reasons. Naturally, there are as many gradations of accompanimental needs between these two extremes as there are dance situations.

The approach to accompaniment varies not only with the differing movement patterns to be assisted, but also with the purposes for which the movement is being performed. A walk, for example, might be part of a warm-up session in the classroom or in the studio where it calls for strict support, or it might be a part of a dramatic dance sequence. In each case the same physical rhythm, tempo, and dynamics may be involved, but the differing movement-intents may demand a completely different type of accompaniment in order to assist in inducing the desired response in the onlooker.

The accompanist's duty is to provide strict musical support where it is needed, and complementary or contrasting support when the situation calls for it. Constantly the accompanist must be aware of strict

phrase lengths as well as fluid or individually paced "breath phrase" lengths of tension and release points *within* phrases, and of accents and hidden pulses. The dance musician manipulates numerous sounds from a vast grab-bag of rhythmic and tonal devices; from these he must select purposefully and with good taste.

In order to be specific, we have chosen in this chapter to use the design of a more or less common dance class pattern, where a fairly set kind of procedure takes place. It is recognized fully, however, that the purpose and content of each lesson changes with the class goals and its level of ability. This division is used, therefore, for discussion purposes only, and in no way do we intend to imply that the following order or procedure is necessarily the only recommended one.

A good amount of daily technical work is customarily done at the beginning of each lesson; this is often followed by a manipulation of these techniques or movement fundamentals into phrases or sequences. More often than not, the last part of the lesson deals with some improvisational or compositional problem, group or teacher or self-determined.

ACCOMPANIMENT FOR TECHNICAL WORK

The accompanimental technique for the initial or warm-up part of the lesson is basically one of parallel support. The music closely follows the rhythm and dynamics of the movement and tries with all its might to help the movement FEEL light or heavy, percussive or sustained, fast or slow, and all the many gradations between these poles. It is necessary for the accompanist to be well acquainted with the rhythmic structure of the movement sequences; he has to watch closely so that the tempo remains intact. He has to supply the appropriate dynamic and tonal range either on the piano or on other instruments or sound sources.

The difficulty of accompanying warm-ups lies not only in harnessing the tempo and supporting the essence of the movement, but also in respecting subtle and justifiable individual differences which in turn affect the group. Once the tempo has been set, it should be kept intact *if possible,* but it is the accompanist's task to make constant slight tempo and dynamic adjustments as the situation calls for them. Therefore it is imperative to *watch the group and NOT the instrument!* It is almost self-evident that the accompanist or a group of accompanists must keep a constant eye on the dancers, even at the expense of musical finesse.

The Alert Accompanist Watches Both Teacher and Class

The Accompanist Who Plays for Herself Instead of the Class

The Technique of "Filling In"

The basic or underlying beat is first established by the class and then is reproduced by the accompanist in a parallel fashion. After this pulse becomes well stabilized, the accompanist often employs the technique of "filling in." Any repeated movement sequence tends to gather momentum, and after not too long a time a walk will become a run unless it is *anchored by accents* and *held back by tones* between the steps. It is therefore imperative to keep the desired tempo steady by "filling in" tones between the actual movement beats.

Naturally the accompaniment is *started* with something reasonably close in scope to whatever is being done in movement, but (though the underlying beat always remains intact) after several measures, the melody may include many more tones. This not only keeps things under control, but also adds an interesting tonal development to a repeated movement sequence. "Filling in" can be achieved by keeping the bass on the piano rhythmically parallel to the dance movement and having the treble digress, or it can be accomplished by keeping a drum or other percussion beat steady and "filling in" by humming, singing, or whistling an improvised tune.

Vocal "Fill In"

We shall refer to the use of the voice throughout the following pages. By this we do not mean that it is necessary for either the teacher or the accompanist to be a talented vocalist. We do mean, however, that the voice should be used to indicate a melodic pattern. This comes naturally to every human being when he hums or syllabilizes. For example, as the drum establishes the underlying beat for a walk, it is easy for the voice to "fill in" as it chants: "And/TAdedeTA a/TA dede TA TA/DUM dede DUM dede/DUM DUM," and so on. The more skillful one becomes at this kind of syllabilizing, the more effective the percussion accompaniment will sound, and much better results are achieved in dance movement.

Counting, which is at best an inferior crutch and a potential bore, is reduced in importance by this method of vocalization. More often than not, the teacher starts the accompanimental pattern vocally anyway; he may say, "And skip and skip—higher and higher" and so on, chanting in the exact rhythm and tempo which are required with the intent of predicting them to the class and/or to the accompanist. This is, of course, an excellent beginning for the continuous vocal "fill in" and the syllable-chanting just discussed.

Choice of Instruments

It is important always to have a group of instruments convenient whether a professional accompanist is available or not. The piano is a very versatile instrument for it has a large tonal range; it can produce dynamic degrees from legato to staccato and from pianissimo to fortissimo. It also serves **excellently** as a percussion-orchestra type instrument. Nevertheless, it has its limitations. ANY instrument or prolongedly fixed group of instruments is potentially monotonous. The ear is apt to become insensitive more quickly to a more restrictedly toned instrument, as for example the

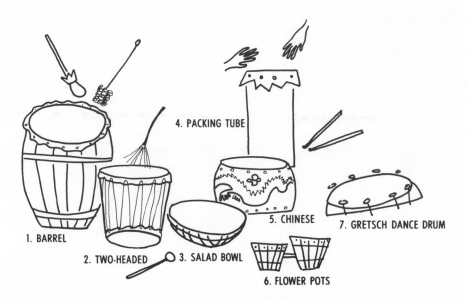

A Variety of Drums

1. BARREL
2. TWO-HEADED
3. SALAD BOWL
4. PACKING TUBE
5. CHINESE
6. FLOWER POTS
7. GRETSCH DANCE DRUM

widely over-used drum, than to the many-sided piano, but even the piano can be overemployed.

The choice of instruments for accompanimental purposes during this part of the proceedings (warm-ups) is largely determined by the tone length or the tone duration of the sound source. The tone length should be matched fairly closely to the step length, or if the movement is axial, to the movement duration. In other words, the accompanying tone should correspond in time duration to the amount of time that the foot rests on the floor during locomotor activity, and it should correspond to the duration time of the axial movements.

Since high pitched percussion instruments are short-lived in tone duration, they do double duty for high and light type sequences. Woodblocks or triangles are good choices of instruments to use for accompanying runs or skips. These not only produce the desired tone length, but also supply an illusion of height and speed via our mental associations, for we tend to link high tones with speed and lightness.

Drums are very satisfactory dance accompaniment devices. They range from the small high-pitched group to the large, double headed barrel types and the kettle-drums. There are also some very efficient portable drums which are especially satisfactory when used by the teacher who furnishes her own accompaniment.

Any drum can produce several good tones. The drumhead responds differently when it is played near its center or its rim, if it is struck by the lambswool or the wooden portion of the mallet, or if it is played with the hands. It can produce a woodblock-like sound when hit on the base or outer portion, and a scraping sound when the mallet is run across the tacks which secure the drumhead. It is a good idea to have several sizes of drums available in order to obtain a variety of pitch and resonance.

Gongs are extremely effective in certain technique situations, but they are a bit less easily controlled dynamically than most other percussion equipment. However, a wonderful job can be done with gongs in helping some sustained dance movements, and gongs are sometimes used to accompany slow falls and recoveries. Their job is usually more restricted to compositional work.

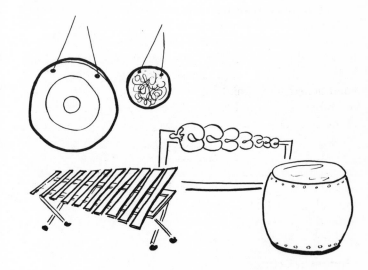

Gongs, Xylophone, Temple Blocks, African Drum

Then there are bells, rattles, sandpaper blocks, woodblocks, and tambourines, all of which are suitable for accompanying quick, sharp, or vibratory types of movements.

There is of course no set recipe or prescription to indicate which instrument should be used when or where. There should, however, be variety, and in this

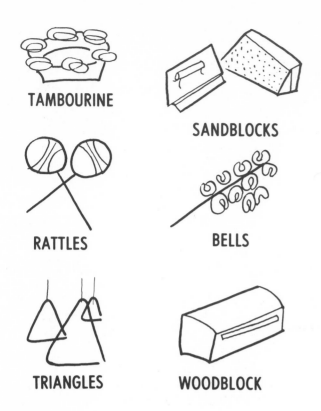

TAMBOURINE

SANDBLOCKS

RATTLES

BELLS

TRIANGLES

WOODBLOCK

Examples:

When the accents fall on *unexpected* beats, we have SYNCOPATION. A simple example follows.

Instead of this:

Try this:

Even and Uneven Patterns

To distinguish between rhythmically equal and unequal values as far as succeeding step length is concerned, the dance jargon has put labels of "even" and "uneven" upon set repetitive patterns. For example, walks and runs are considered "even" since the foot pattern allows an equal amount of time on the floor, whereas skips, slides, and gallops, which allow less time for the hop than for the succeeding step, are termed "uneven" patterns.

Examples of Accompaniment for Typical Warm-Ups

The following suggestions involve the use of simple percussion equipment. Piano accompaniment techniques are discussed later, and examples of composed piano accompaniment may be found in the last portion of the book.

WALKS

Medium size drums

4/4 or 2/4 depending on how pronounced the **accent** on the third beat is:

RUNS

Woodblocks, triangles, and tambourines may be used for accompanying runs. The voice may also be used in order to add melody. Runs are not necessarily a great deal faster than walks, but they seem speedier because of their lightness. The "filling in" by the accompanist starts almost immediately since more notes

part of the lesson (warm-ups), the instrument should correspond in character to the type of movement which it is to accompany.

Phrasing

More often than not, but not necessarily so, warm-up sequences fall into phrases of four, eight, or sixteen measures. Binary division seems to come naturally to us for we like things that are divisable by two. Our having two eyes, ears, arms, and legs perhaps has conditioned us to thinking that obvious symmetry is a desirable and natural thing. However, the whole scope of modern art, music, and dance is one of off-balance tension and stress, and therefore is not conducive to the traditional eight measure phrase. Nevertheless, during the technical part of the lesson it is often just as well to keep things comfortable and allow the phrases to end predictably. Again, however, there are the important exceptions, and a lively seven measure run will put a spirited accent into the lesson!

Rhythmic Context

The 4/4, 2/4, 3/4, and 6/8 rhythm patterns (or time signatures) are the most common ones which are used during the warm-up period. As is explained under "rhythm" in the chapter on "Elements of Music for Dance," this means that there are a certain number of beats in each metric unit, and that each beat receives a certain amount of time. The first beat of each measure receives a natural or *primary* accent, and secondary accents fall on succeeding beats depending upon the rhythmic configuration.

per measure help to create the illusion of a faster rate of speed.

Vivace

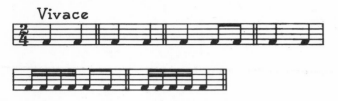

A popular variation of the ordinary dance runs are those performed in 3/4 and 6/8 patterns; these are lilting and often have a Viennese waltz quality.

SKIPS

Either a 2/4 or a 6/8 rhythm pattern is possible here since the two rhythms are closely related by accents occurring in the middle of their measures.

A 6/8

and a triplet 2/4

look and sound almost identical.

It is advisable to employ the 2/4 pattern for a fast, forward type of skip, and to use the 6/8 pattern for accompanying higher, slower skips. Thus:

Skips

hop step hop step hop

hop step hop step hop

A vocal "fill in" is very important in order to add a melodic content which sets the genre of the slides.

Small drums, blocks

Moderato to Allegro

etc.

GALLOPS

With the exception of directional differences, gallops are very similar to slides in their actual execution. Slides usually are performed sideways; customarily gallops are directed forward or sometimes backward.

There is a marked difference between slides and gallops, however, in dynamics and often in tempo. The gallop is in general more boisterous than the slide.

Medium size drums plus cocoanut shells or blocks:

etc.

SWINGS

Since the 6/8 rhythm is essentially "swingy" in character, it is almost exclusively used for every type of swing. A 3/4 will serve nicely, however, on occasion. Melody is essential in accompanying swings, and a very simple piano improvisation is possible here.

Example:

Repeat this pattern, then begin a "fill-in" with the right hand, such as:

etc.

Small gongs are also appropriate for use as accompaniment for swings. Their legato tone is conducive to having the dancers sustain the swing until the next impetus occurs.

A 6/8 basic pattern with a variation of "fill ins" serves well if the pattern is adhered to as an underlying base throughout.

BOUNCES OR BODY BENDS

Again, either a 2/4 or 6/8 pattern may be employed for accompaniment, depending upon the nature of the bounces. Crisp, sharp ones are best accompanied with a 2/4 base, whereas the swingy, more relaxed bounces seem to invite a 6/8.

Small to medium size drums, and the voice:

or

LEAPS

Leaps take many shapes and forms, are "even" or "uneven" in rhythm, and perhaps are the most difficult of the locomotor patterns to accompany. It is enough usually for the accompanist to adhere quite closely to the basic pattern, and to supplement this with vocal "encouragement." The accompanist has to be on guard to match individual differences in tempo, for the performance of leaps is apt to vary considerably as a result of different body builds. Short-legged people will "land" sooner than long-legged ones, and men usually attain higher elevation than women.

TURNS AND FALLS

Turns and falls vary so in kind and in execution that they need to be accompanied in a rubato fashion, unless they are strictly set by the teacher, or have a disciplined rhythmic and tempo base. ("Rubato" means "time robbed or stolen.") When accompanying turns and falls, the metrical time frequently has to be modified or adjusted in order to parallel the movement.

ACCOMPANIMENT FOR MOVEMENT FUNDAMENTALS

As the lesson becomes more complex, more thought, planning and effort must be given to the accompaniment. Whereas the accompaniment for warm-up is necessarily fairly rudimentary, that for the second part of the lesson requires more planning. This part of the lesson usually includes more locomotor or axial *sequences* (or *combinations*). These may have been previously worked out by the teacher and then taught to the group, or they may be developed by the students and teacher during the lesson.

Accompaniment for movement fundamentals might be either parallel or complementary, or it might vassilate between these. If the sequence is technically difficult or rhythmically complex, it is best to help it along at least at first by adhering accurately to the rhythm, tempo, and dynamics indicated, thereby closely translating the movement into a kindred sound sequence.

If, on the other hand, the sequence is geared mainly toward dynamic expression (or a "quality"), a looser type of accompaniment might serve well. Contrast can often accomplish what imitation cannot. For example, an excited movement phrase might well be supported by a quiet or essentially withdrawn sound background. This is similar to holding a blotch of color against a contrasting background in order to evoke a real awareness in the onlooker of that which he is meant to perceive. Sometimes a single repeated tone on a triangle can be excellent music for a frantic series of turns!

It is the accompanist's job to determine the right technique for each movement sequence. With experience, he decides to use parallel or complementary sounds, produces the proper tone color from well-chosen instruments, and he senses when it is time to change patterns. He never loses sight of the group and always receives his clues from it. Therefore, it goes without saying that he needs to be placed strategically in the room.

ACCOMPANIMENT FOR BEGINNING IMPROVISATION

The purpose of the third part of the lesson usually is to give experience in creative expression. Perhaps the class and the teacher have decided upon a stimulus for composition or for improvisation. Unless a piece of recorded music is used for this purpose, it is again the duty of the accompaniment department to furnish sound. In this case the situation becomes more open, more complex, and perhaps most stimulating. Various solutions to set problems are found by the participants, and so the accompanist has to enhance *each individual study* with appropriate sound. He employs various techniques. Since the studies usually are short and not necessarily thought of as performance pieces, they are "kernels" rather than full-fledged compositions (unless, of course, we are dealing with a class in composition). The music can help to give these studies an aura of wholeness, and of completed form. Usually the accompanist can improvise some kind of adequate music after he has seen the dance pattern once, and often this suffices for a quick presentation.

However, this procedure leaves everything to the creative talents of the musician and does not help the dance students in analyzing their studies in terms of exact phrases, measures, and so on. Ideally, the accompanist should see these simple studies two or three times while they are in progress. Analyzing helps him, but it helps the students even more; it assists them in pinning things down, and they learn in this way a good deal about the musical structure of their dances. If the students are in doubt as to exactly what it is that they are doing (how many measures it takes them to get from one end of the "stage" to the other, or why and when their rhythm was forced to change from a 2/4 to a 5/4 with a couple of 7/4's at Susie's entrance), the accompanist can assist them in understanding these things. A common temptation is to force the whole study or dance into the same tempo or rhythm mold, hardly wavering from beginning to end. While it is perfectly acceptable to have a steady rhythmic or tempo base, it is by no means necessary or desirable, and often is less interesting.

The accompanist frequently takes the initiative while experimentations are in progress and wanders about the studio to watch the progress of the individual dance groups. This gives him a chance to think about the sound he will use for the various presentations, and he can discuss his plans with the students. At the same time he can make the dancers keenly aware of what they are doing phrase-wise and how the music can help with the communication of their ideas.

Chief temptations to the accompanist are those of overusing the piano, doing too much parallel accompaniment, and/or "pushing" or imposing ideas on the group via musical suggestion. It is not easy to avoid any of these errors, but if it can be remembered that the accompaniment is but an integral *part* of the effort, then the accompanist will probably be able to produce an efficiently economical yet sufficiently significant sound score.

OBSERVER-ASSISTANTS TO THE ACCOMPANIST

At almost every dance lesson, a group of observers can be found. It is expected that these persons watch the lesson and take an active part in it by *absorbing*.

Sometimes it is really interesting to observe a lesson, and sometimes it is merely frustrating to sit at the sidelines and not participate. These students can be a great help to the teacher, accompanist, class, and themselves, if they can be used in the accompaniment department. They can have fun playing percussion instruments and/or the piano-percussion; in addition, they can learn much about the principles of music and the dance-accompaniment relationship.

Naturally, the teacher and the accompanist have the responsibility of initiating the members of the class into elementary accompaniment procedures. After a few bangy, introductory sessions it will be found that students become fairly ambitious and selective in choosing appropriate sounds. A feeling of pride and self-involvement as well is achieved if some of the equipment is student-constructed.

Chapter 4

PRECUSSION INSTRUMENTS

Musical instruments may be classified into groups that .are (1) *bowed* (the violin family—violin, viola, violoncello, and double bass); (2) *blown* (the woodwind section—flute, piccolo, double reeds, clarinet, and saxaphone; the brass family—horn and trumpet, trombone, and tuba); (3) *plucked* (the violin family, and the harp, guitar, etc.); or (4) *struck* (the piano, and the percussion group—timpani, bells and chimes, drums, castanets, cymbals, triangle, gong, tambourine, xylophone, etc.). Of all the instruments, the percussion group is the most widely used for dance accompaniment. Percussion instruments provide a variety of tone and color; they may be manipulated in ingenious ways, and combined to give unusual dynamic and artistic effects.

THE PLAYING OF INSTRUMENTS

The technique of playing percussion instruments, or almost ANY instrument for that matter, requires the use of a *controlled, relaxed arm.* Give yourself plenty of room so that the full weight of the arm may be utilized. *The sound should be coaxed OUT OF the instrument* and not pounded into it. Tension is exerted only at the split second when the sound producing area of the instrument is actually struck, after which the arm muscles relax immediately.

If the sound waves emerging from the source were only visible, then the matter of giving them a sufficient life span would be appreciated more readily. It is important to get out of their way! As soon as the desired tone is produced, *the arm must relax AWAY FROM the sound area.* This serves a dual purpose; namely, it assures the production of the aforementioned optimum life of the sound waves which die on contact, and it allows physiological relaxation after the tension at impact which is necessary when striking the sound producing area.

All percussion equipment should be suspended or tilted when played. This can be accomplished by either

LIFT TONE OUT

DON'T POUND IT

hanging small instruments from wires or strings, and manually tilting drums or erecting tripods for them.

THE CARE OF PERCUSSION INSTRUMENTS

The most important thing to consider in regard to the care and preservation of instruments is their vulnerability to temperature changes. Extreme heat, cold, or dampness have disastrous effects on rawhide, of which the heads of drums are made; drumheads expand and contract when exposed to climatic changes. Keep them away from radiators, open windows and doors.

Adequate storage space should be provided for percussion equipment so that it can be hung on racks or stacked neatly away. Drumheads, however, should never be covered by another instrument. *Do not stack*

15

anything on the drums, nor is it a good idea to slide double-headed drums along the dance studio or gymnasium floor; this practice will shortly fray the edges of the rawhide.

Naturally, it is desirable to allow everyone to experiment with the instruments, and it is important to set up a permissive and encouraging atmosphere in which to do it. It might actually be better to sacrifice an instrument to enthusiasm once in a while rather than to be overprotective toward this equipment. Nevertheless, *instruments are not toys,* and they should be treated with respect. Students should be taught how to care for and play them effectively.

THE CONSTRUCTION OF PERCUSSION INSTRUMENTS

Instruments such as drums, gongs, woodblocks, triangles, tambourines and shakers, sandblocks, bells, and so on, are available commercially. Most of them, however, can be constructed easily if budgets require this. Aside from monetary reasons for so doing, however, it is fun and instructive for students to create their own instruments, and they invariably produce some wonderfully unorthodox concoctions which supply unusual tone color for unique dance sequences.

Excellent directions for the building of simple percussion instruments have been published in some recent books on elementary education. While most of these instruments, which are designed for use in rhythms classes in the kindergarten and early primary grades, are often toy-like, they do have great value in early musical and visual motivation. Though they must be sturdy, they need not last for years, for children are fond of change and are stimulated by new groups of equipment ever so often. The authors of this book, however, strongly feel that for purposes of dance accompaniment, the main core of the percussion equipment should be very carefully constructed in order to assure good

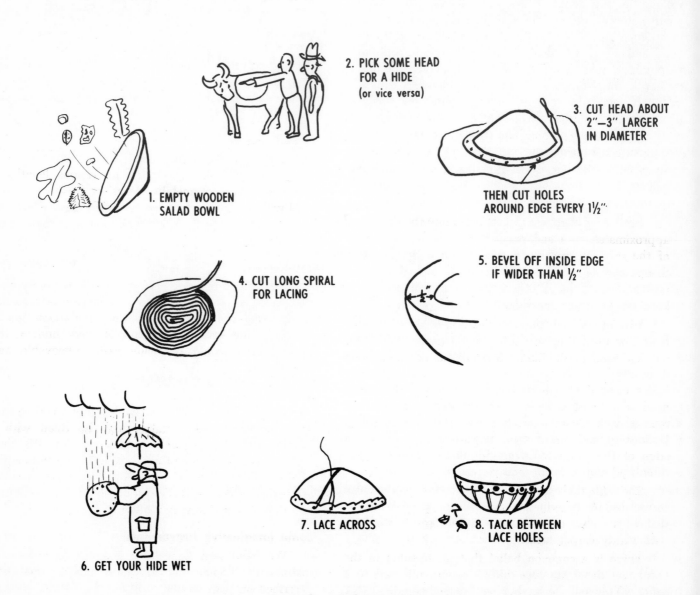

1. EMPTY WOODEN SALAD BOWL

2. PICK SOME HEAD FOR A HIDE (or vice versa)

3. CUT HEAD ABOUT 2"–3" LARGER IN DIAMETER

THEN CUT HOLES AROUND EDGE EVERY 1½"

4. CUT LONG SPIRAL FOR LACING

5. BEVEL OFF INSIDE EDGE IF WIDER THAN ½"

6. GET YOUR HIDE WET

7. LACE ACROSS

8. TACK BETWEEN LACE HOLES

To Make a Salad Bowl Drum

resonance, and also to save time and money in the long run. Professional instruments are therefore desirable, but it is also quite possible to construct some percussion equipment that is very usable and of high standard. Some suggestions are presented below.

Single-Headed Drums

A warning before you start! Use only sturdy *rawhide* for drumheads. We have experimented with chamois, innertubings, airplane glue on muslin and parchment, and other such materials, but have found the results disappointing and, at best, only temporary expedients. A well constructed drum can give good service for years, and it therefore pays to invest in a good drumhead.

A wooden base of the weight and size required (a small instrument produces a high tone, and a large instrument gives deep resonance); a piece of rawhide which overlaps the base by a good two inches; these, plus tacks and/or thongs are needed. Wooden kegs, butter tubs, wooden buckets, hollow logs, and wooden salad bowls make fine bases. If offered a choice, buy rawhide which was obtained from the section that was the animal's back, since this seems to be the sturdiest part of the hide (deer skin, goat skin, sheep skin, calf skin, etc.).

Ways of constructing a drum are described below:

1. Secure the body for the drum and clean it. If the rim of the base is too wide, be sure to bevel it down before starting. The rim should not exceed one-half inch in width; if it does, it will be found impossible to stretch the drumhead to its fullest capacity.

For lacing purposes, punch holes into the drumhead approximately one and one-half inches from the edge of the rawhide, and about two inches apart. Leather thongs may be purchased or they can be cut in spiral fashion from a piece of rawhide. It is important to keep the lacing in one piece!

Soak the rawhide and the lacing in water for several hours, or until they are soft; then squeeze the water out and smooth the skin. Stretch the rawhide while it is still wet evenly over the drum base and start lacing back and forth on the diagonal until the drumhead is fastened securely. Always stretch tightly, but remember that leather shrinks considerably when drying. Upholstery tacks may then be driven in around the edge of the drum to give additional security to the drumhead and/or for decorative purposes.

2. With the exception of the lacing process, use the procedure described above. After the rawhide is soaked, stretch it over the base and tack it on the base with sturdy carpet tacks.

There is a common belief that an opening in the bottom of the drum base adds a round, full tone to a drum. This may be so, but we are not certain. ANY change in an instrument alters its tone, sometimes for the better it is true, but this is not always the case.

Double-Headed Drums

A drum with two drumheads is assured of great sonority. Very good double-headed drums can be constructed from nail kegs. Unfortunately, nail kegs are rapidly disappearing from the scene and are being replaced with compressed cardboard containers. Ask someone at the neighborhood lumber yard or hardware store to save for you the ones that are left.

Remove the top and bottom pieces of the keg, stretch the wet drumheads over the two ends, and either lace the drumheads together or tack each one separately to the base.

Triangles

Triangles may be fashioned from dowel rods or curtain rods. Various tones can be produced by suspending different sized triangles.

Woodblocks

Ideally, woodblocks should consist of several narrow, laminated layers of wood. A simpler, though less effective, way to construct a woodblock is to fashion it from one piece of hardwood. An opening is necessary for resonance, and holes are needed to accommodate the strings or wires that are necessary to suspend the instrument.

Xylophones

A xylophone may be made from a wooden base—resonance chamber over which lie various lengths of wood or pieces of metal. Occasionally an ambitious soul will patiently cut the pieces to the sizes which are necessary to produce an eight-tone major or a five-tone (pentatonic) scale.

Sandblocks

Basically, sandblocks are woodblocks with handles; the "faces" of the sandblocks are covered with sandpaper which may vary from a fine to a coarse grade. Since the life span of sandpaper is very limited, the playing area should be made easily removable and replaceable.

Shakers

Gourds, boxes, tin cans, bottles—any wood, metal, glass, or cardboard container—may be filled with a number of things, such as small marbles, BB shot, gravel, beans, rice, or other cereals, or a combination of any of these. A rattle sound is thus achieved. Gourds are perhaps the most successful of any of the containers, and they usually are very attractive.

Some Imaginative Instruments

We have seen some very imaginative, successful instruments. Some of the more unique ones are described on page 18.

Instruments Made from Utensils and Other Objects

1. THE "LELE" GROUP (All three instruments sounded very good indeed!)

A *"Unilele"* (contraction of the words "uno", meaning "one", and ukulele) consisted of a small, round metal base (actually a part of an outboard motor!) onto which was attached a sturdy piece of shaped redwood which resembled the neck of a ukulele. A good sized hole was punched into the top to accommodate a lever. A ukulele string was stretched from the lever over a bridge to the body of the instrument. By tightening or relaxing the grip on the lever, a great variety of tones was produced. This instrument was, in essence, a miniature edition of the favorite "gut bucket".

An instrument called a *"Percolele"* was made from the bottom of an old percolator; grooves were made in its rim to hold ukulele strings which were secured on a thread spool at the handle of the pot.

A *"Gourdelele"* was an interestingly shaped gourd which gave the appearance of a conventional stringed instrument. The gourd was hollowed out, painted on the inside, and equipped with a small bridge, ukulele strings, and tuning pegs.

2. THE BAMBOO GROUP

A piece of round palm driftwood served as a resonance base for a successful instrument. Onto the base, various lengths of sturdy but hollow pieces of *bamboo* were dropped. This instrument had an excellent tone and could be played by a minimum of two persons simultaneously. It gave the listener an impression of an Oriental orchestral sound.

Several good *flute-like instruments* that we have seen were fashioned from green bamboo reeds which had been hollowed out. Strategically placed holes made possible the production of a variety of tones.

Bamboo sticks were made by cutting strips in the tops of two pieces of bamboo. Interesting sounds were produced by scraping against the strips and by hitting the pieces together. Bamboo sticks are good for making hitting, slapping, or scraping sounds.

3. GONGS

Gongs have been fashioned from large pieces of metal which were suspended. Heavy potcovers also produce good sound, but the authentic Oriental gong tone is not easy to simulate.

4. ONE MAN BAND INSTRUMENTS

A *One Man Band* instrument was made from a barrel drum with attachments that included grooves for the production of scraping sounds, a woodblock, a piece of sandpaper on either side, and bells suspended from the rim. This instrument was fun to have.

5. OTHER SOURCES OF SOUND

The classroom, studio, and gymnasium are full of potential sources of sound. Striking any part of the walls, metal or wooden surfaces, or running mallets across radiators or venetian blinds, results in perfectly acceptable, unique accompaniment.

THE PIANO AS A PERCUSSION INSTRUMENT

The piano is perhaps the most widely used instrument that provides music for dance in our western culture. This is almost inevitable since the piano is such a generously endowed piece of musical equipment. It possesses a vast range of tones and a grand palette of tone colorings within a dynamic scale of fortissimo to pianissimo, legato to staccato. It is, therefore, a rather independent instrument for it can deal with all the musical ingredients simultaneously.

The dance accompanist uses the piano as his "home base", playing it in the conventional manner by depressing the keys and pedals, or sometimes in a less orthodox fashion by playing with mallets on the strings and the metal or wooden portions of the instrument. Then there is the "prepared piano" which alters the original piano tone into new, percussion-like sounds. The latter makes an important contribution to the area of composition and improvisation.

Different People will make Different Instruments

Interesting Sounds from Unusual Sources

Too often the use of the piano is left to the professional accompanist exclusively, and both teacher and students take it for granted that the instrument is "off limits" for them. They associate Bach, Bartok, and improvisational talent with it. And well they should, but this should not be the extent of its usefulness. Nor should we consider that the piano is merely an excellent accompaniment aid simply because it is put into the percussion orchestra group. While the drums are often blatantly overused in dance classes with little respect for, or sensitivity toward, their place, the piano more often than not stands in the corner unused except for social or folk dance classes, unless, of course, a professional accompanist is available.

Following are some beginning techniques for piano improvisation which are geared mainly toward an uninitiated group, that is, toward persons who do not play the instrument but have the natural musicality common to all who dance.

A fairly simple beginning toward using the piano as "just another instrument" is to start with two people at the keyboard. One brave soul will tackle the bass, another the treble. The person on the left should start the proceedings by firmly striking out the basic rhythmic patter of that which is to be accompanied. Never mind the chords at this stage. Courage! One gets a "feeling" for pleasing and interesting combinations with experience. When the pattern has been established, after a half or full phrase perhaps, the person on the right should start with a fill-in technique. It might be best to *start* and *end* phrases on the note C (see chapter on notation) in order to give the dancers a feeling of musical punctuation (phrase endings).

If things get a little out of control, it might be best to stick to the black keys exclusively. A more restricted and musically reminiscent melodic and harmonic pattern can be achieved by that technique, although the penta-

Playing the Inside of the Piano

tonic mode of the arrangement of the black keys eventually sounds rather monotonously "oriental".

If no partner can be found for the initial experimentation in this kind of piano improvisation, use a drum or tap the piano lid with the left hand in order to produce the underlying beat, and do the filling-in portion with the right hand on the keyboard.

We have found that persons with some, or even a good amount of piano playing experience, usually are the handicapped ones when it comes to such keyboard improvisations for dance. They clutch on to conventional chords and little melodies which are pleasant enough but are too conditioned by the sound of "Ruthie's First Piano Book" or a smattering of Tschaikowsky, to do much good for a modern dance sequence of any kind. Of course, we are not advocating a "hit or miss", completely-at-random activity after the first experiments have been completed, but until one gets one's bearings, that is still preferable to little saccharin flavored tunes or to an underlying beat that is not maintained.

The pianistically oriented person needs some "undoing" but, of course, no discarding of that which he has learned. His more agile fingers will do him excellent service, and that which he has learned about harmony and other musical principles will stand him in good stead. His main problem will be that of freeing himself musically and getting acquainted with modern textures and his own creative potential.

There is a wonderful working area for the production of sounds in the inside portion of the piano. There are strings that can be plucked or struck, and there are numerous metal and wooden portions which may be used for added percussion sounds. Lambswool, wooden and metal beaters, as well as fingers, whole

hand or fists, may be employed. The pedal, extreme right, is very helpful in allowing the percussion sounds to "hover" for a longer time, and a particularly interesting effect can be achieved when a tremolo sequence is being rumbled out on the bass strings, after which the pedal is released very gradually.

Although this kind of piano percussion is more often reserved for the "creative" part of the lesson, it has its place in the warm-up sequences as well. There are stretches, for instance, which can be accompanied beautifully by running a hard mallet across the treble strings. Seems to do something to the vertebrae!

If a particular pattern is to be played on specific strings, it is best to mark these strings which have been selected with colored chalk.

The Prepared Piano

As the term implies, a prepared piano is one which has been altered before it is played. The purpose of the preparation is to change the quality of the conventional piano tone in order to give the instrument an additional dimension in sound. The American composers, Henry Cowell and John Cage, are credited with being among the first to use the prepared piano.

When objects are placed upon the piano strings, the timbre of the instrument is changed so that it sounds slightly more metallic, more percussive, and less true in pitch; the traditional piano timbre, as a result, becomes almost unrecognizable. The degree of tone alteration naturally varies depending upon the nature, character, and weight of the objects which are placed on the strings and with their particular arrangement upon them. After the strings have been prepared according to the plan, the pianist plays the instrument by depressing the keys in the customary manner.

Elaborate percussion-ensemble effects can be achieved by placing various objects on the strings— wooden blocks, heavy cardboard, metal objects, books, and so on. The bass strings can bear heavier preparation than the lighter, shorter treble strings, both from the standpoint of tolerance and effectiveness. Strings which are altered must be marked carefully so that performances can be duplicated.

For both a *general* or *partial* preparation, it is necessary to make a thorough analysis of the arrangement of the strings on each piano, for instruments differ. Metal bars and cross-bars vary in design. For these reasons, no chances should be taken when, for example, a performance is moved from the rehearsal studio to the concert hall. The size and weight of objects must be tested on each individual instrument and in order to achieve the same effect on a different piano, objects sometimes have to be regrouped or substitutions made.

A piano may be prepared by another method. Instead of weighting the strings, thin strips of wood or metal may be wedged between two of the three

A Prepared Piano

strings of a given note. This arrangement results in a bell-like tone when the piano keys are depressed.

Interesting results can be achieved by combining the prepared piano with the piano-percussion playing technique which was discussed previously. It will be remembered that this requires one person at the keyboard utilizing the prepared areas, and another person, standing, using mallets on the free strings.

The piano preparation methods which are described above may be used more satisfactorily on a grand than on an upright piano; some inventive things, however, can be accomplished on the latter. Since gravity works against one in this situation, obviously the objects cannot merely be placed upon the strings; they must be fastened to them. Masking tape, or some other similar material, may be used for this purpose. A more reliable way of producing the desired sound, however, is to have two or three persons hold the objects against the strings. This can be done successfully, of course, only after the individuals have practiced pressing the objects against the strings correctly. Naturally the front panels of the upright must be removed!

Compositions written for the prepared piano usually are notated by means of the conventional piano method

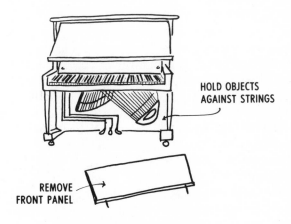

Preparing an Upright

but explicit directions for the preparation of the piano are also included in the score.

All this may arouse some serious frowning, or at least questioning, with regard to possible damage to the instrument. All we can say is that unless the piano is painstakingly cared for, the above activities do not harm it nearly as much, for example, as placement of the instrument near an open window or radiator.

Chapter 5

MUSICAL NOTATION

The development of musical notation (the translation of music into visual symbols) has been the result of a slow, evolutionary process. It is considered probable that the first attempts to represent sounds by graphic methods were made by the early Chinese and Hindus. It is known that the ancient Greeks had a highly developed system of modes or scales, and concepts of harmony. Their system of notation was closely related to the Phoenician letters and alphabetical symbols, but there remain today only clues as to the actual music of that time. Interpreting the past through a study of present primitive usage is a commonly employed method, and luckily, through this means a considerable amount of traditional music has been kept intact in certain localities via ancestral heritage, that is, father teaching sons (for example, in Africa and in Asia). Another rich source of information about the past is gained from the liturgy of Orthodox religious services.

During the development of music as both a sacred and secular art, a gradually fixed notation system became established, and today we depend upon this particular collection of conventionalized symbols to describe specific rhythmic and melodic directions, namely NOTES. Our present Western notation system was invented and expanded chiefly by Catholic priests and monks within the period ranging from the early Christian beginnings to the thirteenth century and beyond. It grew from the use of dots, dashes, curves, and so on, and from the use of melodic markings above words in texts and hymns. It developed slowly from the use of these markings and from various colors which were employed to designate certain notes, and from some symbols for time duration, to a system of diamond shaped figures which were placed on lines and which combined to give both melodic and rhythmic directions simultaneously.

In the eleventh century, Guido of Arezzo changed the system to a staff of five lines and utilized the four intervals or spaces in between the lines as well. The innovation so improved the then existing method that this Benedictine monk often is called "the father of modern music." Fixed scales, based upon the Grecian modes then evolved, and with them, the musical rules of combining tones melodically and harmonically. During the Renaissance and beyond, when the dance again assumed an important role within the Western secular arts, two of these former Grecian modes, namely the Aeolian and the Ionian, became the more popularly used because of their structural "anchorage points" which were then, and are now conducive to music for dance. In these modes some tones are lighter in value and some are heavier; as a result they have different weights or importance and this makes a resolution possible.

So invaluable has musical notation become that a rather curious and illogical development has resulted. Whereas originally the system was recognized to be and continually developed as only an *aid in the communication* of music, it has by now become so well associated in the minds of people with music per se, that practically no musical education, or the playing of music by professional or amateur is considered possible or feasible without the use of "notes." Playing by ear or improvising are considered highly skilled musical adventures. Indeed in most cases, the notation system is taught first, before any other effort is expended to acquaint the learner with music. This does seem to be a rather roundabout way of establishing contact with an art form, as perverse a process perhaps as expecting or even requiring children to learn to read before allowing them to speak. Illiteracy is definitely not an asset, but it does not deprive the individual of an appreciation of the meaning or the beauty of words.

The notation system is a splendid tool for recreating (reading) and creating (composing) music, but it is only a means of representing sound by symbols, that is of putting sound into writing. The system is not infrequently limiting since it is based rhythmically on strict mathematical devices, and melodically on the exact placement of tones; as a result, certain important subtleties are ruled out in both cases, and especially in the melodic area. For instance, there is no way to record quarter tones, those sounds which lie exactly between half steps (between "C" and "C sharp" for example), tones which are most important in Hindu and other Eastern musical cultures. Nevertheless, the value of the now highly developed system of notating music cannot be overestimated and it has opened the door to music for almost everyone who wants to "read" sound.

Since the dancer and the dance teacher must deal with music constantly, it is very desirable that they acquaint themselves thoroughly with the notation system. This not only facilitates communication with musicians but simplifies the analyses of musical scores. Being literate in the official language of recorded sound makes it easier to determine the exact structure of a composition which is to serve choreographic purposes, and certainly mutual accomplishments and interests are furthered between dancer and composer when language barriers are overcome.

In order to make the learning of notation a bit more palatable, the process has been put into the form of elementary piano lessons below.

RHYTHMIC SYMBOLS

As was stated earlier, RHYTHM is essentially a series of pulses or beats which divide time into certain units, or MEASURES. ACCENTS, or stresses, which occur repeatedly give an inkling of the metric unit, that is, whether there are 2, 3, 4, 5, 7, or 6 beats per measure. Therefore, at the beginning of nearly every piece of music a TIME SIGNATURE is given; this tells us what to expect. Three-four time (3/4) means that there are three beats in each measure, and that a quarter note (♩) receives one, the basic underlying beat. A quarter note is worth one-fourth of a whole note, the unit upon which the rhythmic subdivisions are based. In a like manner, the time signature 4/4 indicates that there are four beats per measure with the quarter note receiving the basic beat, and 6/8 means that there are six beats in each measure with an eighth note (♪) receiving one beat. The symbols look like this:

Notes

The *whole* note is indicated in this manner:
If the time signature is 4/4, count 1-2-3-4 for the whole note.

The whole note may be divided into two *half* notes:

The half note may be divided into two *quarter* notes:

The quarter note may be divided into two *eighth* notes:

Single eighth notes are written ♪ or ♩ depending on where they are placed on the staff of five lines:

They can be combined in groups of two or four in this manner:

The eighth note may be divided into *sixteenth* notes, thus:

EXERCISES:

A. Learn to recognize, and clap or beat the following examples. It is suggested that the total pattern be looked over first; then reduce it all to the smallest note value. In other words, count "ands" and "and-a-s" when there are eighth and sixteenth notes involved, so that the tempo can be maintained throughout the more complex measures.

1.

2.

B. Compose your own rhythmic examples in 4/4 time.

Dots Following Notes

A dot following a note increases the value or time length of that note by half of its original metrical weight; a dot following a quarter note  prolongs its value by that of an eighth note, for example:

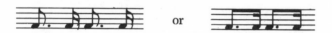

An eighth note followed by a dot is increased by the value of a sixteenth note, as follows:

EXERCISE:

A. Learn to recognize, and clap or beat the following examples:

Exercise 1

Exercise 2

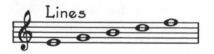

Rests

Rests in music are carefully planned, calculated rhythmic *silences*. Each note value has its equivalent rest symbol, and rests are named, as are notes, in terms of time duration.

| Whole | Half | Quarter | Eighth | Sixteenth |

EXERCISE:

A. Learn to recognize, and clap or beat the following example:

MELODIC SYMBOLS

Melody is a series of tones arranged in succession. A meaningful melody is one that is so constructed that it gives a feeling of form, and therefore it is understandable to the listener. Ordinarily, melodies are based upon a system of scales or modes which are patterns of successive tones placed a certain distance apart.

Our Western scales are remnants from the Greek modal systems and employ eight tones. The intervals are based on a fixed scheme. In the major scale all the tones are an equal distance apart with the exception of the third and fourth and between the seventh and eighth steps; in these two cases the tones are only half the regular melodic distance apart. In the minor scales, "half steps" occur more often and there is, in addition, an augmented, or a step and a half, between the fifth and sixth notes.

A system of KEYS OR KEY SIGNATURES emerges from this order and, depending upon where the "tonic" or first note of the scale occurs, the dreaded SHARPS OR FLATS are encountered, but the latter help to keep intact the order of the whole and half steps.

Staff

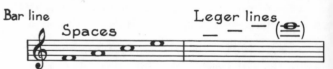

The musical staff is composed of five lines and four spaces. Vertical lines across the staff mark off equal measures of time; they are called *bar lines*. Often it is necessary to add *leger* (or ledger) *lines* above or below the staff in order to extend its range.

Clef

The clef is a symbol used in musical notation which denotes the position and pitch of the scale represented on the staff. The *Treble Clef,* which is indicated by the character ⎨𝄞⎬ , includes the higher or lighter tones, and the *Bass Clef,* 𝄢 includes the lower or deeper sounds.

As has been previously explained, the form of a note indicates its relative length, such as a quarter or an eighth note, but the pitch or tone of a note is recorded by its position on the staff.

Treble or G Clef

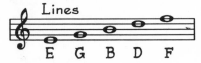

Lines

E G B D F

Treble or G Clef

Spaces

F A C E

Bass or F Clef

Bas Clef

G B D F A

Think ahead one line or space

G
F becomes

B
A *etc.*

EXERCISES:

A. Learn to recognize and to know the names of the notes on the lines in the treble clef—E - G - B - D - F (*"Every Good Boy Does Fine"*).
B. Learn to recognize and name the notes on the spaces in the treble clef—F - A - C - E (*"Face"*).
C. Learn the notes in the bass clef.

Piano Keyboard

The pattern of notes on the piano keyboard is composed of a continuous repetition of eight tones in a certain order, growing higher in pitch to the right and lower in pitch to the left. The white keys are tuned to whole step intervals with the exception of E - F and B - C where half steps occur. The black keys are used for the additional half steps previously mentioned.

The note "C" is located directly to the left and underneath the two black keys 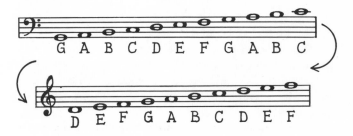. It is

G A B C D

followed by notes D - E - F - G, after which are notes A and B. A note on a line is followed directly by a note on a space. It is wise, therefore, to learn the notes in direct succession as they occur on the keyboard (C - D - E - F - G - A - B - C), as well as by their places on lines and in spaces (E - G - B - D - F, and F - A - C - E), for it is necessary to recognize notes immediately.

G A B C D E F G A B C

D E F G A B C D E F

EXERCISE:

A. Learn the keyboard notes and their corresponding placement on the staff.

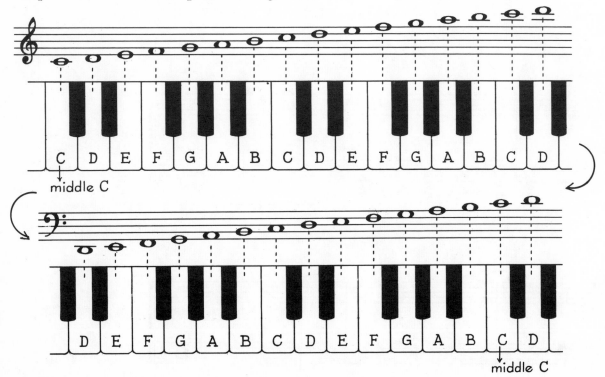

C D E F G A B C D E F G A B C D

middle C

D E F G A B C D E F G A B C D

middle C

The piano essentially is a percussion instrument. Its tone is produced by striking a string with a felt hammer. As a key is depressed the hammer which is attached to it rises and strikes, and as the key is released the string is touched by the "damper" to silence the tone.

There are three pedals, two of which have the function of sustaining tones. The pedal on the extreme right lifts the "dampers," a series of felt attachments which deaden the tone after the string has been struck. If they are not allowed to descend upon the strings immediately, then the tonal resonance is allowed its full span. As soon as the pedal is released, the dampers come down upon the strings thus automatically extinguishing the sound and allowing the next tone to be heard clearly by itself. The middle pedal, the "Sostenuto," holds the damper of one note at a time (or a series of simultaneous tones; i.e., a chord), thus allowing one particular note or chord to last while the music goes on. The left pedal works somewhat differently on various pianos, but its main purpose is to soften or diminish the dynamics of the music; for this reason it is often referred to as the "soft pedal."

The pianist must play with the full arm and allow himself sufficient space to do so. The weight of the total arm should be utilized so that a round and full tone may be achieved without "cramping." The pianist should sit forward on the piano bench in order to secure optimum leverage.

The pianist's fingers are numbered 1 - 2 - 3 - 4 - 5 with the thumb being number one in both hands.

Accidentals

An accidental is a sharp (), a flat ( ), or a natural ( ); these signs occur before a specific note and are directions to change the pitch to one that is different from that indicated by the signature or by a change that was previously made.

The change indicated by an accidental holds true throughout the remainder of the measure in which it occurs, but this change is automatically cancelled in the following measure.

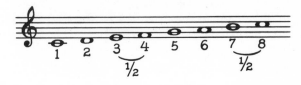

Scales

Key signatures in Western music are based on major and minor scales (Diatonic).

C MAJOR SCALE

EXERCISES:

A. Learn to play these patterns:

1.

2.

A MINOR SCALE

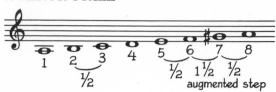

"Keys"

Keys are based upon the first, or the *tonic* note of the scales.

D MAJOR SCALE—all F's and all C's are sharp.

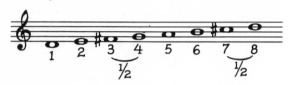

Key Signature:
2 FLATS

All B's and all E's are flat.

Sharps

Key of: G   D   A   E   B

Flats

Key of: F   B♭   E♭   A♭   D♭

EXERCISE:

A. Learn to play the following:

A little Polka

Chapter 6

TEACHER-ACCOMPANIST RELATIONSHIPS

The role of the accompanist in the classroom seems to fall roughly into one of the following three categories: (1) a second class citizen relegated to the corner of the studio; or (2) a bossy know-it-all; or (3) the good-to-ideal helpmate and professional partner of the dance teacher.

Observations indicate that the third of the above categories is unfortunately more the exception than the rule. This may be partly due to the fact that too many mediocre musicians have settled for having to "bang out music for dance", and they consequently take very little pride in their work. They find it uninteresting and barely profitable and, in turn, the dancers they accompany form the same opinion about that which is offered them. The situation might be called an "accepted stalemate" in many instances, but that is really too easy a way to shrug off a situation.

One of the most important reasons for this professional dilemma is the fact that too few good musicians who are interested either in accompaniment or composition, are attracted to being active as *dance musicians*. They take a good look at the situation, and on the surface it seems as though the musician is always SECONDARY to the total effort. In classes, he seems to *serve* the "goings on" (and the terms "serve" and "servant" can be closely associated psychologically!); at the concert or recital, he is in the pit or backstage, and at this time the visual element is far more important to the audience than the audible. Why, therefore, should he devote himself to *this* artistic endeavor rather than accompany violinists, or singers, play in ensembles, or, if he must stay semi-obscure, write music for films or television?

The answer is not simple, and a good bit of spadework must be done by dancers, dance teachers, present professional dance accompanists, and dance composers to orient their creative musical colleagues to the very real merits of this field. Dance is by its very nature so closely related to music that working with it, composing for it, and yes, serving it, holds pure joy for the initiated.

Unfortunately, the whole situation is too often handicapped by the fact that dancers are seldom millionaires, and can pay only very limited amounts for scores and minimum fees for classes. There are musicians who would like to enter this field, but feel that they could afford it only as a sideline, for financial reasons. However, many schools now have allocated reasonable budgets for full-time accompanists but even so, well trained persons are still needed to fill these positions. The problem is therefore not entirely economic in scope, nor is it entirely a problem of recruitment.

Because of the numerous problems involved in hiring and working with an accompanist, many dancers and teachers have learned to get along without "live" music. Recordings, which are often highly useful, nevertheless have qualified advantages. They have been overused, as has the trusted old drum which instead of being employed as a limited substitute, has become THE instrument for modern dance accompaniment. Many a dance teacher has confessed that she would be at a loss to know what to do with an accompanist if one were provided!

This means, of course, that a whole integral part of the "stuff of dance" has become neglected or virtually ignored, and whereas the ballet has leaned perhaps too heavily upon music for support and for inspiration, the modern dance, on the other hand, frequently suffers from a lack of good musical support. Either is unhealthy!

WHAT TO LOOK FOR IN A DANCE ACCOMPANIST

Job interviews are so often centered around the word "experience" that we might as well start with it too, if only to give ourselves a chance a bit later on to dwell on the advantages of lack of experience.

We shall, therefore, begin with that which might be considered the ideal situation.

The Ideal Accompanist

A very good, experienced accompanist should have had, first of all, sound professional musical training parallel to that of his dance colleague, and an academic background equal to that of the person with whom he will be associated. These requirements are not only important because of the work, but they make possible a good partnership psychologically since equal schooling commands mutual respect.

Secondly, the ideal accompanist should be well versed in dance terminology and be familiar with some typical lesson progressions. He, of course, should have facility in improvisation and composition, and he should be articulate in music analysis. But most of all, he must take a genuine interest in the progress of the dance group and in the individuals involved. The latter requirement is naturally to his advantage since the job would be far from interesting otherwise.

Ideally, the accompanist should have done some dancing for he needs to be able to feel movement imaginatively. It helps immeasurably to know just how much tension a certain stretch requires, or what a leap "feels like", and that certain movements need to be clothed in very elastic rhythms and dynamics. He can, if he has had even a small amount of dance training, empathize with the dance movements he is accompanying because he has developed a kinesthetic awareness of them.

The very good accompanist is also a flexible person who adheres to a minimum number of hard-as-nails theories. Naturally he is dedicated to his artistic convictions and should share them verbally and musically. However, partners can exchange ideas on an even basis without compromising their beliefs, and they can learn from each other in so doing. We simply mean that an excellent dance accompanist is interested in that which his dancer-colleague is doing and gets excited about it, even though perhaps his former experience has been with a topflight artist whom he considers to be marvelous! He should not be completely sold on the G-technique or the H-technique of the dance, nor should he consider S to be the only modern composer worthy of note.

It is most important that a warm, friendly relationship exist between the teacher and the accompanist, and therefore the ideal collaborator in this common enterprise is one whom you like and respect as a human being as well as a creative artist and co-worker. Each has a separate but mutually dependent function to perform in the total creative process.

From the accompanist's point of view, the ideal arrangement also includes the following: a GOOD piano situated in a strategic spot in order to afford maximum visibility; good percussion and recording equipment; and signals that have been mutually determined in order to allow things to run smoothly.

The accompanist also is most anxious to be involved completely in all of the class transactions. This means having a part in the planning and in the evaluation of the lessons, being verbally included when pieces of music or dance compositions are analyzed and, in general, being regarded as a valuable professional partner.

The accompanist's repertoire should include short, concise pieces of the Pre-Classic, Classic, and the Modern schools. Pianists usually are well versed in the Romantic and often also in the French Impressionistic eras, but need to add a good supply of Pavanes, Galliards, Allemandes and so on, and the simpler, shorter modern works to his repertoire. (For suggestions, refer to the chapter on Resource Materials.)

We are emphasizing the term "short" in the above paragraph, not because "the shorter the better", but because we oppose the practice of "cutting" pieces of music. It is all right to extract a total movement of a sonata for instance but, in general, it is no more legitimate to cut and paste together a composer's work than it would be appropriate to mutilate a painter's still life if, for example, all that was of value to the viewer was the orange in the middle of the canvas. If a composer's work is used, it shoud be used in toto!

There is a distinct advantage in engaging the accompanist on a salary rather than on an hourly basis; this insures a more compact working day and a permanence that is appreciated by both parties. If the salary is fixed for the duration of the school year, then the musician is able to rely with confidence on a known amount to which he may or may not have to add other activities, such as some private teaching in order to supplement his income. His dance accompaniment work at the school is then regarded as an entity rather than as an odd collection of so many single hours at a specified fee per hour. The accompanist's annual salary can still be computed by estimating the hours involved at the school's hourly basis (include not only actual playing time, but composition, shopping for sheet music and recordings, and any other preparations which are necessary to the job).

If the contract is presented with a round salary figure for the year, this will mean for the accompanist financial and professional security, and this plan assures both the dance teacher and the accompanist a long-range working relationship. Not only does this arrangement up-grade the dance accompanist's position, it also makes his status a more official one and recognizes the school's real need for his services.

Preferably the accompanist should be given a position with professional academic status, thus assuring him the prestige and the opportunities accorded other staff members; if this is the case, the accompanist will readily also accept the responsibilities which are inherent in a regular staff position.

The Interested Beginner

There are many teachers and dancers who prefer the eager novice to the experienced professional accompanist for the simple reason that they feel that with patience and an investment of time, a "custom tailored" accompanist will emerge. The beginner we speak of is only a beginner in dance however. He should be well versed musically, perhaps a recent young graduate of a university's school of music, a conservatory or the like. He should be a good pianist who has recently become interested in dance; he should display some promise in improvisation; and he should be a personable being.

The dance teacher would do well to provide this future. accompanist with at least two preliminary experiences which will speed his progress in becoming an excellent dance accompanist: (1) OBSERVATION (imperative!) and (2) MOVEMENT PARTICIPATION (optional, but highly desirable!) This introductory indoctrination period might last only a few days; it might then be followed by more observation-participation interspersed with some actual playing, possibly on the percussion equipment rather than on the piano.

The teacher should orient the musician, before he begins his accompaniment duties, regarding that which he should look for in dance movements. While the teacher is furnishing her own accompaniment during class, the fledgling accompanist may IMAGINE supportive sound, paying particular attention to the specific rhythmic, dynamic, and tempo details which each movement requires. After about a week or two of this, the musician will have become familiar with the general composition and feeling of a dance class, with progressions, and with that which he should like to provide in the way of musical accompaniment. If he has participated in the dance class part of the time and has felt some of the movements as well as simply having witnessed them, this experience will be most helpful since a kinesthetic concept will have been established as well as a purely intellectual one. After all, the musician's sensation of time and rhythm and his feeling for movement come, at their basis, from an inner sense of movement. Music is one way of expressing movement.

The next steps in the shaping of the professional accompanist should be taken slowly and patiently. It is a good idea to avoid having the first practical experience be in the area of improvisation, especially if skepticism has been expressed. Use the musician's pianistic abilities and repertoire, so that he can feel comfortable.

The class might undertake at this point a short project on composition to a composed piece of music. This step would give the accompanist two advantages: 1) he would feel secure in playing something expertly, and 2) it would give the students and him a chance to get acquainted while they analyze together the musical structure and the meaning of the piece which was chosen for study.

Gradually then, turn the supportive part of the warm-up portion of the lesson over to the accompanist. Just as in diving, there is no other way but to jump in all at once! The accompanist has watched the teacher use the percussion equipment, and has possibly watched her make piano-percussion or piano-improvisation sounds; there is an excellent chance that by now he feels he can do at least that well very soon, and much better a little later on! He has become somewhat familiar with the teacher's more or less standard class beginnings and progressions, and he no longer needs to worry about specific rhythms and tempi quite so much. He has begun to sense, in sound or music terms, the length of movement phrases, and that which comprises the kernel of each movement or movement progression. His interest will soon turn from merely being able to follow and keep up with the proceedings, to making his music more and more exciting and stimulating. He should be encouraged, during regular after-class evaluation sessions with the teacher, to experiment with new sounds, with counter-rhythms and such.

A bit later on in the course of the accompanist's development, the problem of the musician's getting *too* involved in what he is doing might, and almost undoubtedly will, occur. His head will no longer be focused on the dancers but on the keyboard, and more interesting music than is needed or desired by the teacher will emerge. This is not really a bad stage, even if it is rather disconcerting. (Refer again to illustrations on page 9.) It should, however, not be allowed to last too long for it might indicate a regression rather than growth; it must be remembered that most often the accompanist's role is to produce musical support for movement and only seldom music per se. The teacher now is responsible for making a decision. Is this ambitions stage a good one in the development of the accompanist and should it therefore be allowed to "run its course"? (There is the possibility that it will lead to richer sounds later on). Or, are things getting out of hand to the extent that the musician needs to be brought back tactfully to the realization of the purpose of the music he is issuing? This is a delicate stage, and it must be handled with skill, diplomacy, and finesse or much will be lost!

It will be seen, in summary, that the teacher can help the dance accompanist by leading him (1) to feel dance movement; (2) to enjoy it; (3) to understand it; and finally, (4) to become discriminating in his choice of musical support for it.

The Case of "Our Wonderful Mrs. X"

Somehow, Mrs. X has been a problem to many of our young and ambitious dance teachers. She often appears in the shape of a lovable, middle-aged lady who has been playing the piano for many years at the school to which our young teacher has come. Mrs. X is an "institution" and everyone likes her. She has seen students and teachers come and go; she is often considered a "mother-confessor" and/or a "character". For years she has been accompanying the dance classes, social, folk and modern, though the modern classes have most likely not been very much more advanced than that which was once called "Natural Dance", a phase which was most valuable in the evolution of dance in education but which has since been overtaken. As may be guessed, music played by Mrs. X is limited to pleasant pieces of the Romantic Period, and her improvisations, if any, are in a similar vein.

Now our young teacher is quite well trained in the field of dance, has some wonderful ideas about improving the program, and feels that certain things require a change. After all, she was employed for the purpose of introducing some new and young ideas into the dance department.

Relations between Mrs. X and our young teacher may be fairly congenial until the first modern dance class session. At this time it is soon made clear that Mrs. X does not approve of changes; she attempts, by word and implication, to convince our young teacher that things have been all right before all this "modern stuff" came along. She thinks discords are very ugly indeed; not only that, but all the movement "gyrations" are not pretty or graceful! Nor does she mind saying so! She says it to the young teacher, to the students, and to the other members of the department. Our young teacher suddenly imagines herself to be a rebel in both Mrs. X's and her colleagues' eyes, and, being young, she either goes overboard in defending her ideas, or, not wanting to be disliked, compromises or indeed abandons some (most) of them.

What to do? As soon as Mrs. X is recognized as Mrs. X, proceed with caution! There is an excellent chance that her attacks may well be disguised curiosity and a combination of ignorance and consequent insecurity toward an idiom she would really like to know something about. It is difficult for her to start studying something new at this stage in her career, so she is much safer in attacking the whole thing.

A subtle orientation period might work. Bring modern recordings and corresponding sheet music to class for her to listen to and play. Involving her in music analysis sessions and asking her to play on the percussion equipment might help. If it can be tactfully arranged, it is usually a tremendous help to have her meet and observe an excellent modern dance accompanist at work.

If, however, every effort on the teacher's part is obviously futile, then it might be best to get along with a minimum of Mrs. X's assistance during the modern dance sessions. The teacher is far better off

furnishing her own sounds, having the students help, and using recordings wisely, than having "Country Gardens" played all semester.

Our young teacher and Mrs. X can still have a fine relationship during the folk and social dance classes where Mrs. X probably does a good job.

The Student Accompanist

Often the school has a very limited budget set aside for dance accompaniment, or even if there is an adequate budget, there is simply no one available to fill the position. In this case, it is a very good idea to recruit some help from the Music Department by asking it to send some of its promising and interested students to the dance teacher.

The students should be screened according to their talent of course, but mostly for their interest in wanting to do this kind of accompaniment, and for their desire to learn about a different type of improvisation and composition.

If the student who is selected feels that he may gain a valuable professional experience, then half the battle is won, and an orientation process similar to the one described under the heading of "The Interested Beginner" may get under way rapidly.

The teacher must realize that music students, and especially composition students, are most intensively interested in the musical material itself and not in its function for another medium. Most likely, the student-accompanist's knowledge of music for the dance is limited to large ballet scores or pieces of music with descriptive dance titles such as Valse, Polka, Polonaise, and so on. Also, it must be remembered that a student may lean either toward composing or improvising in too careful or conventional a style, or toward the experimental, in which case anything conservative seems obnoxiously old fashioned and passé to him. Either extreme is a difficult one with which to deal, but the first pattern may be overcome by encouraging experimentation, and the second by both an acknowledgement of the interesting things produced, and by a request for some steadier music and samples of works of composers of other centuries as well.

The importance of the Dance Department's function as a training center for young accompanists should not only be not overlooked but greatly encouraged. In addition to the real possibility of the emergence of some dance musicians, the resulting interdepartmental relationships are of tremendous value.

CURRENT PRACTICES RELATIVE TO THE DANCE ACCOMPANIST

It may be of interest to explore current practices and policies relative to the dance accompanist; this may shed some light on the nature of this persistent personnel problem and give clues as to how it may be alleviated.

The results of one study indicate that 43% of the high schools in one state included dance in the curriculum in 1953 and in only 15% of these cases was an accompanist employed (mostly students or part-time help); the remainder used record players and percussion equipment exclusively. In 1956, on the other hand, Kinnard found that 45% of the colleges and universities had regularly employed accompanists; however, over half of these were students or part-time accompanists. In contrast to this, Hawkins reported only two years later, that 49% of the colleges and universities employed accompanists (in a few instances, several) on a full-time contractual basis. Conditions, therefore, are slowly improving!

Certain other data reported by these investigators lend credence to that which many dance educators and accompanists believe. Kinnard said that the respondents to her questionnaire (high school teachers) provided this information: (1) "Most dance teachers do not have well trained, experienced accompanists who are capable of enhancing and supporting movement in a skilled fashion; (2) student accompanists receive wonderful training but at the expense of those enrolled in dance classes; (3) record players and tapes are inadequate; (4) only 22% of the accompanists are graduates or majors in the field of music; (5) regularly employed accompanists are needed rather than students or part-time help whose qualifications are dubious; and (6) in order to secure better accompanists, better salaries are indispensable."

From data gleaned from responses from forty-seven colleges and universities throughout the United States in 1958-59, Hawkins concluded: "(1) It is interesting to note some encouraging trends in employment practices that are related to four problem areas (the need for different or more flexible personnel classification, increased status and recognition of the professionally prepared musician, increased salaries and benefits that are comparable to those of the regular faculty, and greater understanding on the part of administrators of the important role of the musician in the dance program); (2) *accompanists in 33% of the institutions have academic or faculty status;* (3) 26% hold academic degrees; (4) 26% of the accompanists are teaching academic classes; and (5) *49% of the institutions employ musicians on a full-time contract basis.*"

Good accompanists are necessary if dance programs are to be effective. *In order to attract and keep qualified musicians* it is therefore suggested that the accompanist (1) be given status and responsibility; (2) be assured a salary commensurate with his training and experience; (3) be accorded the same benefits and privileges as other members of the faculty; and (5) be given an opportunity to assist in the planning, teaching, and evaluation of dance classes.

Chapter 7

CHOREOGRAPHER AND COMPOSER

Music which is especially written for modern choreography must be designed to balance with sound that which the movement represents. The audible and the visual stimuli should be interdependent. Achieving this union is not a simple process, for the composer customarily strives for as interesting, as intriguing and valuable a work as does the choreographer. In the case of scores for the modern dance, however, the music must be composed to serve another medium and cannot as a result often be an entity.

The argument to the contrary, which comes to mind immediately, is that of ballet music. We are all familiar with the lovely, and indeed, very complete musical scores which have been written throughout at least three centuries for the ballet. Composers have been commissioned to create dance music from the early pre-classic through the classic period, from the pinnacle stage in the development of the ballet (the Romantic Era) into the "international" ballet of the early twentieth century, and finally for the "modern" ballet of today. In these cases, the composer was, and is, given an outline of ideas (perhaps a chronological story sketch), and he can then proceed to write a fully developed musical score, having been given virtually "carte blanche" to do so. The composer and the ballet choreographer confer at intervals, but usually the detailed choreography does not get under way until the main body of the music is almost completely structured. The choreographer then works to the composed music, and that is as it should be in the ballet idiom. The story and the thoughts expressed are important of course, but the stage decor, the manipulation of steps, and the spectacle of the total ballet performance are of paramount significance. The accompanimental scores for the ballet, therefore, can be fully orchestral, complete pieces of music per se.

It is perhaps superfluous to say, therefore, that for the majority of composers, writing music for the ballet seems a more gratifying and satisfying creative endeavor than writing music for the modern dance. Not only does the ballet score have the possibility of being performed without the presentation of the ballet, but —and this is no small consideration—the ballet company is more often financially equipped to give an orchestral work a hearing than is the modern dance company. In other words, a ballet score is as complete and performable a piece of the composer's collection as any of the other works that he has composed, but modern dance music is seldom performed independently of the choreography.

Luckily for the modern dance, however, there are quite a few devotees of this art within the fold of contemporary composers. They believe what the modern dance has to say and they enjoy playing an important part in saying it. They are satisfied to assist in creating an artistic balance between the movement and the sound, and if their scores cannot be performed without the dance, it does not hurt their vanity since they are concerned with the overall effect. (Naturally there is some satisfaction derived by the composer from the fact that the choreography is equally helpless without the particular music which was created with and for it.)

The story or the subject-matter of the ballet is often but a pretext for the dances and the music. Contrary to this, the bulk of modern dance choreographies are founded on abstractions, or really extractions, of literal ideas. A chronological story line or a statement of the choreographer's conception of the dance may give the modern dance composer only a rudimentary basis for his work. Consequently, he usually asks the choreographer to work out one or two main movement themes or sequences first, and then the composer creates accompanying sound for the phrases.

Ideally, the whole compositional process should flow from the choreographer to the composer. After the initial choreographic ideas have been mapped out and a beginning has been established, it might be wise to allow the music to go ahead and develop for a while; the choreography then proceeds *to* the music temporarily, but it then should develop beyond that point so that the music again follows, complementing and paralleling the movement ideas. There is thus a see-saw action between the dance and the music, and both the composer and the choreographer strive to further the ideas which are being commented upon. The process is very conducive to the complementary type of accompaniment, but the composer must consider carefully whether a specific movement sequence needs complete sound support, only a few scattered tones, or perhaps no sound at all.

Naturally the above process is not the most common one, since it is painstaking, often difficult, slow, and demands an almost ideal working relationship between the two artists. An additional, very practical problem is posed by the need for space, since obviously this cooperative undertaking cannot be accomplished in the composer's living room! However, this manner of working contributes to the development of a compact and well balanced piece of art for it requires a "give and take" between the artists, and a true meshing of dance and music. Though it moves slowly at times, the method is more than worth the effort. The experience is not only a satisfying one, but usually insures a successful result.

However, the plan outlined above is not the only good one, nor should it be used exclusively even if it is possible to do so. There are at least two other methods of procedure.

There are some dances which need to be diagrammed rather completely by the choreographer before he works with the composer at all. In these cases, the dancer first creates the *general* sequences of the total work and fashions all the important sequences. At this time he presents all this material to the composer so that the latter can then clothe the work in sound. When this is the case, the composer must familiarize himself first with the visual movement themes and their meanings; he must understand the choreographer's *intent* so that he can support that most of all.

In the above situation, it is the choreographer's responsibility to furnish the composer with a detailed outline of the dance and its specific rhythmic configuration. For example, he may give the composer a sketch, such as:

Part A: Three women enter. Slow tempo (metronome indication).

Seven measures of 5/4, followed by two measures of 3/4. Repeat.

Man's entrance. Strong, vigorous, march-like. Seventeen measures of 4/4.

Duet between one woman and the man.

Disturbed, searching, yet lyrical in quality.

Five measures of 3/4, three measures of 4/4, ten measures of 3/4; and so on . . .

In this example, probably the composer would face his first dilemma in finding a transition from the women's dance into the man's entrance without dropping the women's theme altogether. They are still on stage and important, but the man's entrance must be picked up in the music.

The choreographer should leave the composer some lee-way in the measure structure, however. Not infrequently, a musical theme needs further development, or even more frequently, it sounds rather exhausted and repetitious after the twenty-fourth measure. On the whole, though, the dance structure should be followed as closely as is musically possible.

Another method is closer to that of the ballet music procedure. In this case the choreographer has a complete idea worked out. He presents it and the important movement themes to the composer, but the choreography is still in a somewhat nebulous stage—that is, only approximate rhythms, tempi, and so on have been defined. The composer then proceeds to write a complete score which expresses the choreographer's thoughts and incorporates his ideas in sequence. Finally the movements are then composed to the music.

In this situation, as in the previous one, changes undoubtedly will have to be made in certain sections of the score. A difficulty often arises in the accompaniment during the emphatic or passionate sections of the dance. This is because a loud, crashing chord or two expresses a great deal quickly, whereas it takes the dance longer to say the same thing in movement terms. Such problems, of course, have to be resolved, but as a rule in this method of working, the choreographer composes *to* the score which has been previously written but which was based on his general ideas.

Most professional modern dance composers like to have a chance at all three (and other) working methods. The first is preferred perhaps, but there is much satisfaction and sometimes a little smoother sailing in either of the two latter procedures. Naturally, here as elsewhere, individual preferences appear. Some dance and music composers prefer "the big line," that of first sketching and mapping out the total work with broad strokes; others work out small parts or parts of themes, one at a time. There is no right or wrong method. That which counts, of course, is the result and the creative process.

Composers, choreographers, writers, and performers from many media sometimes collaborate on another kind of theatrical presentation, called the Dance-Drama, a highly developed entity revolving around a dramatic concept, a story, or legend. Such a composition is often long and may possibly make up a total evening's presentation. Partly because of this, but largely because they demand a complicated blend of dance movement, music, words, and all other elements of theater, dance-dramas are not as frequently presented as dance concerts. A delicate artistic balance is involved: the story must be told, the dance comments must be made, the music must be independent and yet meet the requirements of dance accompaniment. Each medium must communicate that which it best can offer at the proper moments in the drama, and yet all together the whole presentation must make for "good theater."

Chapter 8

MUSIC FOR THE DANCE PERFORMANCE

Under ideal conditions for a dance concert, it could be assumed that there is an unlimited budget from which to draw, excellent theater facilities, an enthusiastic well trained performance group of dancers, a professional musician-composer who serves as musical director, musicians, stage technicians, and designers, all of whom are experienced in the preparation of a dance performance. As it stands, however, the authors have never encountered such a situation and will therefore dwell with a realistic eye on that which is usually found.

First of all there is, and should be, a tremendous difference between the professional dance concert and the educational institution's concert, not always in the performance itself, but always in the *purpose* for giving the performance. The professional artist must be concerned with the final product; the presentation of his works must be paramount. Everything—the music, lights, staging, décor, costume, program arrangement— must contribute to his purpose. In the educational situation, on the other hand, the *process* is more important than the final product, though certainly the best achievable performance is strived for. While the whole performance should be conceived and carried out as artistically as possible, it must be remembered that the participants in a student concert are concerned with *learning about* performances. Nevertheless, though the objectives for performances vary, and the difference between a professional performance, a quasi semi-professional college group concert, and a dance recital by a high school modern dance club is quite pronounced, there are certain considerations which are similar for any dance presentation; these should be observed, regardless of the level of choreographic experience or movement skill.

We will not elaborate on these general criteria for dance performances since they have been covered adequately in numerous publications, and since this chapter is devoted to but one aspect of performance,

namely, music for concert dance. However, it seems appropriate to mention a few general points about balance and theatrics since, in the final analysis, these also affect the kind of music that will be selected for the dance concert.

BALANCE AND THEATRICS

Arrange the program so that there are enough "light" dances interspersed between the tragedies. An audience needs relief from the seriously dramatic as well as from the hilarious. Beginning dance groups in particular seem to lean very heavily upon the dance-drama, soul-searching, overly dramatic types of choreographic ventures, and if no one anticipates the barometer reading, the final concert may easily become stormy indeed! Balance is necessary, balance not only in the kind of dances and, therefore, in the kind of music, but also for variety's sake, there should be trios, solos, duets and large group numbers included in the program.

Lights, stage sets, and costumes, as well as music, help to set a mood and are used for emphasis. Dance needs to be interestingly lighted, but beginners should remember that the prime purpose of lights is to provide visibility, sufficient visibility at all times and in all parts of the theater (house). The purpose of costumes, no matter the level of performance skill, is to enhance movement characteristics and to assist in suggestion. For student performances, a basic dance dress or leotard with tights, to which allusions in the form of color, line, or design accents are added, are most effective, desirable, and appropriate.

CHOICE OF MUSIC

The purpose of music for the dance concert is essentially the same as that for any dance presentation whether it be on the stage, the classroom, or studio. It exists to further, enhance, complement, and stimulate.

Surely there must be a better place for the piano!

Balance and excitement may be achieved by many natural means:

A. The music may be specially and carefully composed for some of the dance compositions.

B. Special attention may be given to variety in tone color; this may be achieved by employing various combinations of instruments and by using both sparse and full scores.

C. Some musical compositions may be chosen for choreographic comment. This means that parts of the total music which is performed are independently playable or listenable, and possibly less intellectual in concept.

D. There may be accompaniment which consists of spoken words, either poetry or a specially arranged "word score".

E. The music might indeed sometimes be a LACK of sound, or "silence". In this case, the movement of the dancers' feet, the breathing of the performers, and even the audience's coughing all add up to partially planned and partially accidental music for the dance.

RECORDED VERSUS "LIVE" CONCERT MUSIC

The music should be alive and therefore be "live". Recorded sound, though occasionally unavoidable, somehow deadens a performance. There is little excite-
ment about the "presentation" of sound which was previously performed and recorded, or at least there is only as much suspense and excitement about it as there would be were the dances presented to the audience as films. It is conceded, naturally, that a Rubinstein recording or a Martha Graham film are exciting, but foolproof renditions on records remove the suspense of watching and listening to "live" performances.

When recordings are used, there is the additional problem of having a really good sound system available; mediocre reproduction results in distorted and scratchy sounds. However, the greatest objection to the use of recordings is not the mechanical sounds that they issue or the mechanics of operating them, but the *kind of recordings* which are so often chosen for use. Too frequently, lush orchestrations and a profusion of sounds, very familiar pieces, and the so-called semi-classics are selected to be "danced to". The essential purpose of music for the dance, therefore, is completely overlooked, and the whole performance, as a result, is in danger of becoming "a music concert with dance accompaniment" instead of the opposite.

Naturally if there is no other way, then it is certainly better to rely on good recorded sound than on poor, or no music. But when recorded sound is used, it should be recognized that an important factor is lacking, and great discretion should be exercised in the choice of music.

MUSIC AS A STIMULUS FOR CHOREOGRAPHIC EFFORT

If previously composed pieces of music are used as a stimulus for dances, then certain factors should be considered:

A. For choreographic purposes, the most successful pieces of music are ones that are fairly cleancut and clear formally. They give the choreographer a chance to either adhere to and parallel the structure of the music, or to go against it, thereby making a contrasting formal statement upon it. (For example, if the musical A theme returns, the dance's A theme might do likewise, or it might make a different statement thus creating dramatic or structural tension).

B. Music which is not absolutely complete or potent within its own right leaves the choreographer more room for action. The score should have "spaces" in it which allow the choreography room to "dance through". Economical and concise works with subtle and varying rhythm and tone color are most desirable.

C. Music which sounds extremely inviting to dance to, the kind that makes feet tap and is usually referred to as being very "dancey", is dangerous for modern choreography. It, and the well known popular variety of music, should be avoided as a general rule for these reasons: (1) The choreographer and the dancers must compete with preconceived specific or hazy dance images in the audience's "inner eye"; (2) Since the music is so very "dancey", it has to a large degree fulfilled its dance purpose already, and a specific choreographic undertaking almost always proves disappointing; and (3) Too often a large part of the audience feels that it would have envisioned some other treatment of the music, thus again the choreographer must compete with distinct preconceived ideas.

D. Avoid the temptation of using too many instruments or too full sounding a score, either "live" or recorded. Unless the dance really warrants it (and there are some notable exceptions in the modern dance where it was important to use full orchestra), it is advisable to stick to small chamber ensembles, piano(s), percussion, voices or other small, carefully assembled instrument combinations. (Some knowing people insist that there should not be more people in the orchestra pit than there are on stage!) The main reason for this elaboration is again to point out that the music must never overpower the dance idea. A great orchestral piece has already expertly conveyed everything that it needs to say and asks for no additional artistic comment.

PLACEMENT OF THE MUSICIANS

There are two possible areas in which to locate the dance-musicians: (1) backstage in the wings section, or (2) in the orchestra pit. (If the performance is staged in a high school gymnasium, then the musicians must be placed in such a way that they may see the dancers but do not obstruct the audience's view.) There are advantages and disadvantages to both the backstage and the pit locations in terms of comfort, visibility, and accoustics.

Backstage

Many dance musicians prefer to be placed backstage not only because from this location it is possible for them to view practically the total stage, but also because there is a chance for mutual signalling at crucial points during dances. Signalling (for beginnings, new entrances, or occasional changes of tempi) is frequently important and necessary, and the closer together that the dancers and musicians are placed, the easier it is to work out these communications.

The backstage location has, however, at least two distinct drawbacks: (1) If more than a grand piano and two or three other instruments are involved, the area gets crowded. Furthermore, the musicians become distracted by excitedly whispering dancers who are about to make their entrance or who have exited on the piano side of the stage. The musicians have trouble concentrating on the playing; it is upsetting to them to have to "shush" the dancers and it is frustrating to the latter not to be able to blow off steam; (2) There is also an accoustical problem backstage. Chances are that no matter where the music is placed backstage, much of the natural resonance is absorbed by rows of heavy borders, drops, and "legs" which hide the instruments. The audience, as a result, hears a diluted version of the actual sounds unless microphone amplification is employed, and unless that is skillfully done, the music might be in danger of sounding recorded.

The Orchestra Pit

Although the pit poses some visual problems, it is on the whole the more satisfactory location for musicians during a dance concert. Usually it is large enough in size to hold comfortably all the musicians and their equipment. Because it is in front of the proscenium, the sound is projected directly into the auditorium and is perceived the way it should be. Signalling, of course, is still necessary, even more so. A buzzer or blinking light system may be used to notify everyone of readiness, both on stage and in the pit.

The pit must be raised high enough so that the musical director has a view of the stage, and, although it is perfectly all right for the audience to see the musicians, the latter's activities and especially the height of the instruments should never obstruct the view nor detract from the stage. The piano lid should be removed completely.

Some of the more recently constructed theaters have electronically controllable pits which may be adjusted to any height by the mere pressing of a button. Since such an ideal arrangement is rarely available, he traditional pit must be "built up" to an extent which llows the desired visibility for musicians and audience. f the pit is approximately the height of the auditorium loor, it may be left at that height. Many high schools ave auditoriums which are arranged in this fashion, and the arrangement works out very well for dance recitals. Since most high schools have fairly adequate auditoriums, the authors are left with the question, "Why are so many high school dance performances held in gymnasia"?

Chapter 9

ACCOMPANIMENT FOR FOLK DANCE

A brief consideration of accompaniment for the folk dance is included in these pages for two reasons; first, much of the music for the modern dance is based upon the folk idiom; and second, supplying music for the folk dance itself makes different demands upon the accompanist than have been discussed so far. Folk dance, like folk music, is the result of a basic instinct for expression; authentic folk arts are handed down for generations and the collaborators whose work they represent, are unknown. Folk dance is in essence a spontaneous movement response or comment upon the style and steady rhythm of music, and both the music and the dance closely resemble one another in structure and in flavor.

THE FOLK DANCE ACCOMPANIST

The folk dance accompanist must have an extensive repertoire of basic folk dance music. He must be familiar with the fundamental folk patterns, such as the waltz, the schottische, the polka, and the mazurka; and he must be at home with various commonly performed national dances. In addition to being well acquainted with this material, it is very important that the accompanist be able to play with verve, and with a flair for the folk idiom. He must *always* keep the rhythm of the dance and give the music a spirited quality.

Creativity on the part of the accompanist is limited to nuances in interpretation when patterns are repeated. He may, for example, change the key occasionally; he may make some harmonic alterations of the "original;" or, now and then, he may make slight variations on the main theme. However, that is all that is required or, indeed, wanted. Rhythms and melodies should be played authentically; they must not be distorted. Folk dancers, as a rule, do not welcome noticeable changes from the familiar and the traditional. The aim of the accompanist should be to recreate old and familiar material with spontaneity and with great respect for the culture that it represents.

Neither the folk dance accompanist or teacher, however, should worry unduly about violating anything in musical literature. Existing folk music usually consists of authentic melodies and rhythms, but when these are published, simple harmonic basses have been added, and it will be found that these basses differ depending upon the publication. The accompanist, therefore, has the right to alter these to suit his needs. It does no harm even to play only a skeleton, harmonically, provided that the melody and the rhythm and the tempo are correctly executed. The accompanist-teacher will have to learn to give upbeats (such as "Ready-And" or similar verbal signals) for starting, and will have to learn to call out the next movement figure while still completing the previous one on the piano. The main thing is to *keep playing* or singing if things get a bit rough pianistically. Dancers will forgive a wrong note much more generously than the stopping of music to correct it, or the hesitation which might be required in order to hit just the right note. The motto is "Keep going in the right tempo!"

As a rule, it is best to acquaint students with the music almost immediately. After they have heard it, the teaching of the steps and figures becomes more meaningful. The music should be heard as much as possible all throughout the teaching process. Humming, singing, "lateda-ing" and simple piano playing should be employed until the dance is practically learned, and then a recording may be used at the end for "dessert."

There are a great many good recordings available in the field of folk dance. Indeed, there are very few dances which are not yet recorded. Here, contrary to our discussion on recordings for modern dance accompaniment, recorded sound is welcome since the tone color of folk dance instrumentation is so very valuable. It is interesting and exciting to dance to the sound of the accordion, the zither, the flute, and the typical folk ensembles since the timbres of the instruments so often represent the very essence of the music. Of course it still holds true that, whenever possible, "live" music should be provided for folk dance demonstrations, symposia, and the like, but the piano alone is not an ideal instrument for some folk dance or folk music reproductions. The piano simply does not have an old or sufficiently rustic sound.

In teaching, however, it is still most advisable to have a pianist available. Recordings are inflexible and everyone tires of the constant sameness in the music which the record issues. When teaching a dance (and especially in the slower, sectionalized approach at the beginning of the learning process when tempi are slower and repetition is in order), it is much better to work with an accompanist who can adjust rather than be limited by a recording. After the dance has been learned, the recording will be received by the dancers with enthusiasm because of its authentic tone color.

If no accompanist is available, it is quite possible for the teacher to learn to play simplified versions of some of the folk dances which he plans to use during the course. He can play at least the melodic and rhythmic line (see Chapters III and V), and ANY one note indicated in the bass chords of each measure will do for accompaniment of the melody.

DEVELOPMENT OF BASIC FOLK STEP PATTERNS

Since at present there is a lively Renaissance of folk dancing and of folk music in the United States, it might be interesting to explore the origin and migration of folk dance material from Europe to America.

The absorption of folk material into the various art idioms is an important factor in any national culture. It is not uncommon to recognize the nationality of a composer by his thematic material. Music sounds German, Russian, or Polish often because Laendler, Slavic melodies, or Mazurkas are woven into the musical structure. The influence of ethnic material cannot be underestimated; hence it might be appropriate to review

not only the original patterns, but to see how these patterns relaxed when they were brought by immigrants to this country.

It is generally accepted that the Waltz, the Polka, the Schottische, and the Mazurka patterns serve as the basic step patterns for most of our Western folk dances. We shall, therefore, explore each as to origin, rhythmic configuration, style, and movement design.

The Waltz

The origin of the waltz as a social dance form has long been a subject for animated discussion among musicians and dancers. It may be traced with ease to its folk dance ancestors—the Drehtanz, a round or turning dance, and the Laendler, a popular couple dance in three-quarter time which apparently was born in the villages of Southern Germany and Austria. But the process through which the original boisterous, step-hop type dance became transformed into the flowing, elegant Viennese pivot-like glide is debatable. It may have been affected by the Allemande or the Menuet. The latter provides perhaps the more plausible explanation because of its three-quarter rhythm and general similarity to the waltz.

However the Allemande could very well have influenced the waltz since it was a sentimental dance which was executed in a gliding manner with couples facing each other. The dance which preceded the classic waltz was often referred to as "Deutsche" (German) or "Allemande" (French, meaning "German"). Probably credence should be given to all of the explanations, and there is no real reason for dispute regarding the evolution of the waltz for it is always difficult to trace accurately the development of any social or art form. People are seldom aware, at the time, that they are involved in a period of transition; when a particular form finally crystallizes, memories of its evolution are not always dependable with reference to the exact sequence of its emergence.

The waltz was a favorite of the people before it was admitted into the formalities of the court; Queen Luise of Prussia is credited with introducing it there in the late eighteenth century, and horrified many in so doing. Suffice it to say that in its classic form it became most fashionable and conquered all of Europe in the nineteenth century. Its capitol was undisputably Vienna, where it was nurtured first by composers such as Schubert who wrote many beautiful waltz melodies, short lilting three-quarter compositions with an emphasis on the first beat of each measure. These little Waltzes are charming descendents of the Laendler and they were meant to be listened to as well as danced.

With the arrival of Josef Lanner and the elder Johann Strauss, the Viennese Waltz came into its own, swept the ballrooms, and scored a grand victory over all who took exception to the fact that it was a couple dance shockingly executed in that which we now blandly and nonchalantly call "social dance position." Johann Strauss Junior is considered the supreme master of the form and took the waltz movement to its peak—a virtual waltz craze. We are still enormously devoted to all of his music, but especially to the swaying, lilting ingeneous waltz melodies which he created.

The essence of Viennese Waltz music is the three-four rhythm, played at a very lively clip. The tempo is often interrupted by a phenomenon called "hesitation," a temporary halt or suspension, which by the principle of contrast, makes the return to the original speed even more exciting than it was initially. The hesitations are never written into the score, but are improvised by the performer or the conductor.

Viennese Waltz melodies are light and graceful; they have grandeur and sweep, yet they are often reminiscent of Tyrolean folk tunes or, indeed, yodels because of large jumps which characterize the melodic intervals. The principal step pattern of the Viennese Waltz involves a pivot turn per measure. The turn is initiated by a pronounced body-lean toward the intended direction of movement.

The classic waltz continued to be popular in Europe and was eventually "imported" to the United States. It is interesting to note, however, that although the Viennese Waltz was taught in its courtly form in the large cities, a new, slow style labeled the "American Waltz" emerged. A single sharply accented bass note on the first beat of the measure, followed by chorded second and third beats is a characteristic of its accompaniment. The regular, even, three-quarter pattern is played slowly enough to allow a step on each beat.

Waltz (even)

step step close

It is believed that this change of pace and the difference in genre may well have resulted from the Western movement. The open plains, and the simpler "dance halls" were more conducive to the unpretentious American Waltz than to the fancy, polished, and very fast Viennese.

There was a most interesting throwback from this development incidentally, for an "English Waltz" or "Slow Waltz" later appeared on the European ballroom scene in the early nineteen-twenties. This version combined the hesitation aspects of the Viennese Waltz with the slow tempo of the American, and enabled dancers to perform a fairly elegant waltz within the crowded space of present day ballrooms.

The Polka

The origin of the polka is traced to Czechoslovakia where the name denotes "Polish Girl." Again, however, as in all questions of folk or social dance ancestry, quarrels exist. Poland? Czechoslovakia? Nevertheless, a Balkan or Bohemian origin seems undisputable.

The polka is a lively dance performed to spirited, melodic music in a two-four rhythm. As a folk dance, its step pattern is "hop-step-together-step."

Polka (uneven)

Hop step together step hop

The pattern is "uneven" because of the quick tempo of the upbeat (the hop) in comparison to the other movements.

The polka, like the waltz, is found in many European folk dances and is used as a basic structure underlying the travelling patterns of specific dances. Not unlike the waltz, but to a less extreme degree, the polka also invaded the ballroom and remained quite intact in its social dance form, but it has been embellished and elaborated upon by composers. Johann Strauss wrote innumerable polkas, and so did Smetana and other Czech composers. The fact that the polka lends itself so well to humorous musical treatment or comment, has stimulated many modern composers to experiment with its pattern for the purpose of combining levity with distortion.

Again, the shift from Europe to the American scene resulted in a relaxation of the dance pattern. The first thing which was omitted was, of course, the hop. The polka presently became a Two-Step, and as a result, this dance became "even" in its rhythmic character.

Two step

Hop step close step hop

The Schottische

According to some musicologists, the schottische ("eccossaise" in French) is a French dance, or a dance which the French interpreted as a Scottish dance, hence its name. The dispute, therefore, among dance and music scientists revolves around whether the dance really was originally of Scottish origin or whether it began as a French interpretation of a Scottish dance.

The schottische is an "even", comfortable, though animated dance with a basic pattern in four-four time with a secondary accept on the fourth beat. It invites many simple, yet pleasing variations of the original step pattern, which reads like this:

Schottische (even)

Run   R   R   hop

Uncountable folk dances have the schottische as the basic pattern.

The schottische never quite reached the degree of popularity which either the waltz or the mazurka enjoyed in the nineteenth century ballroom, but it definitely was a welcome addition to the social dances of the period, not only because it has a charm and dignity of its own, but because it offered relief from the athletic demands of some of the other dance forms.

Needless to say, the form of the schottische was not altered after its importation to the United States. Its commonest variation, that of adding a step-hop measure after the basic step-step-step-hop sequence, seems to have emerged as the official schottische pattern in this country.

The Mazurka

The mazurka is easily traceable to Poland, where a group of peasants, called the "Mazurs," gave birth to the dance form called the mazurka; this became the Polish national dance. Here we have a vigorous, interesting pattern which unlike the waltz, polka, or schottische, consists of several movement designs. Probably this is due to the fact that the mazurka involves the rhythmical eccentricity of shifting accents within its boisterous three-four rhythm. A sharp accent sometimes falls on the third and often on the second, in addition to the customary first beat. A mazurka pattern might look like this:

or like this:

or it may consist of a mixture of accent patterns throughout the piece:

Mazurka (even) shifting accents

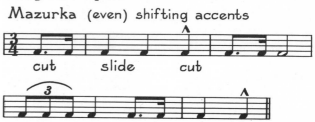

cut   slide   cut

The step sequence, or step pattern, is variable also, but its recurring figure is the "coupé" or "cut" step taken to the side:

coupé slide close   or   coupé hop hop

Another vigorous, spirited variation is known as the "Polish Mazurka". It consists of a sideward leap, stamp or forward slide, and step.

leap stamp step   or   leap slide step

The mazurka in idealized and elaborated form became a great favorite of the ballet. It has verve, elegance, and vigor. It is composed of a fiery, forceful pattern that is easily enlarged into a technical tour de force for the main soloists of any classic ballet.

The mazurka became the "Varsouvienne" in America. The term, Varsouvienne, itself is traceable to Warsaw, Poland. The original coupé step became simplified in our country and the boisterous hop was eliminated, but the pattern is still quite recognizable; in this version the coupé amounts merely to a pointing of the foot toward the other leg at midcalf level.

Chapter 10

A BRIEF HISTORY OF MUSIC FOR THE DANCE

It would be presumptuous to assume that the vast and immensely rich field of music history could be covered in a few pages, and it is not our intention to attempt to do so. We merely wish to present for the dancer and the dance teacher a brief review of the development of music, focussing on its relationship to dance. This we feel is desirable for three reasons: (1) The choreographer uses music and therefore needs to be acquainted with its background and characteristics; (2) The dancer usually welcomes help in discovering sources of accompaniment; and (3) It is of interest to note not only the influence that music has had on dance, but also that which dance has exerted on the development of music.

The choreographer does depend to a large degree upon pieces of music which were composed before his choreographic ideas were born, and it is therefore necessary that he be familiar not only with the structure and the dynamics of the selected musical work but, in addition, the period during which it was created. A musical composition written in the eighteenth century obviously demands a different treatment in style of movement than a modern work. The choreographer must be familiar with the general genre of the historical period in order to comment upon it intelligently or to abstract it. This knowledge should by no means detract from the joy of simply experimenting or improvising at random to an appealing piece of music of any historic origin. However, the conscious and intellectual awareness of function, style, purpose, and form of the era and some knowledge of the specific composer's work are valuable and necessary bases for choreographic comment or for the selection of appropriate dance accompaniment. When one is creating to a piece of music, he is probably not attempting to mirror the music with a movement parallel. But many ballets are adapted to, and many dancers choreograph, precomposed music; the process amounts to a visual accompaniment (though no exact paralleling

of idea or movement is hereby intended). In this case it seems self-evident that one ought to know what it is that one is accompanying.

Dance has exerted a very considerable influence on the development of music during the years, and it continues to be an important stimulus for contemporary composition. The dancer should be acquainted with the main composers of the important historic intervals in the growth of music literature so that he can easily find appropriate music for his purposes. In addition he needs to know the names of contemporary composers, particularly those who have worked with dancers, in order to uncover further sources of stimulating and congenial new material.

Roughly speaking, the history of Western music falls into the following categories:

Monodic Music: Pre-Middle ages up to 800
Polyphonic Music: Approximately through 1300
The Renaissance: Through 1500
The Baroque Period: 1600-1750
The Classical Period: 1750-1820
The Romantic Period: 1820-1900
The Twentieth Century: 1900-

We shall treat each period briefly, mentioning musical characteristics of the time, pointing out representative composers, and noting especially the dance developments of the age. A more detailed analysis is given to contemporary music. Since dancers are particularly interested in current musical developments, a subsequent chapter is devoted to the growth of the modern style and to a listing of twentieth century composers.

In general, it will be seen in the following pages that two diametrically opposed concepts have dominated the evolution of music. The history of music (and of all the arts for that matter) is characterized by movements toward and away from these two aesthetic ideas: (1) *The Classical,* which is distinguished by formality, emotional restraint, objectivity, and adherence to structural principle and pure form; and (2) *The Romantic* which openly expresses subjectivity, personal feeling, freedom of form, and sensuality. These two trends often coexist but usually the scales are decidedly weighted in one direction. Before an era can produce its grandest and culminating artistic figures, the seeds of the opposing revolutionary idea usually have started to grow.

MONODIC MUSIC
(Pre-Middle Ages to 800 A.D.)

In our Western culture, music prior to and during the Middle Ages (and into the Renaissance) generally is referred to as "Music in the Christian Era." Music of this period falls into two principal divisions, those of *sacred* music (plainsong) and *secular* music (folksong). The first category includes liturgical musical offerings while the second embraces all music other than that used in religious services. The most distinguishing feature of all musical antiquity is monody. Music gradually developed from the early chantlike "monody" (that is, music limited to one voice at a time, or a single melodic line) to "polyphony" (music which employs two or more voices or melodies simultaneously).

The most famous of the early sacred monodies is the Gregorian Chant which can still be heard in Roman Catholic services today. It has an intriguing and beautiful quality, and is of particular interest to the dancer, for its rhythms do not fall into any set repetitive sequences because they were composed to fit the elastic rhythms of the words of the text. The Gregorian Chant is classical in its simplicity and modesty, its restraint, clarity, and melodic severity.

Coexisting with plainsong was a secular musical art. The secular monody of the Middle Ages was preserved and performed largely by traveling minstrel groups, the Provençal troubadours and the trouvères in France, and the Minnesinger in Germany. These musical poets, often of aristocratic birth, sang ballads, dance songs, courtly love songs, laments, and romantic tales of foreign lands. The performers often improvised accompaniments for their texts and employed richly diversified musical forms.

Fortunately, examples of the works of these singers are extant and are recorded in "L'Anthologie Sonore," a series of records that are available from The Gramophone Shop, Inc. Following are names of some of the composer-performers of the Middle Ages: Betrand de Born, Adam de la Halle, Blondel de Lyle (Troubadours and Trouvères); and Wolfram von Eschenbach, Heinrich von Rugge, Walther von der Vogelweide (Minnesinger).

POLYPHONIC MUSIC
(Approximately through 1300)

Sometime after the early Middle Ages a practice of immeasurable influence began, that of singing plainsong monody in two parts simultaneously a fourth or fifth apart. Polyphony thus started from a simple parallel singing of the same melody by baritones and basses moving in a parallel motion. This kind of elementary polyphony was called "simple organum," and from it gradually evolved more and more complex intermeshing of melodies, all of which eventually came to full bloom during the Renaissance (called the "Golden Age of Polyphony"). The peak of polyphonic literature was reached with the unsurpassed harmonic consonances of the Bach era. Since harmony predominates in Occidental music, this innovation—organum—is considered by some to be the most significant single creation in the whole history of music.

Related developments during this period which are of concern to the choreographer include the appearance of the rondel, a polyphonic form which made possible the later contrapuntal devices of imitation and the canon. And the fifteenth century mastery of counterpoint added such compositional techniques as augmentation and inversion. Secular music also was amplified and strengthened by an increasing number of unpretentious but virile and spirited folk dance forms.

Important composers of the period include John Dunstable and Guillaume Dufay.

THE RENAISSANCE
(Through 1500)

The sixteenth and seventeenth centuries have been of particular interest to dancers because of the rebirth at that time of the art of the dance as an accepted artistic and social endeavor. Dance was introduced into the court as a prescribed social function, and since composers were commissioned by their aristocratic and royal patrons to write dance music, they drew inspiration from the popular dances of the day. Dance has always been a source of stimulation for musical composition but it must be remembered that, for several previous centuries, dancing was not permitted by the dignitaries of the Church. Only the folk forms survived, as they always will, and they became the basis for the gradually evolving court dances.

During this time it was customary to pair dances, performing two which contrasted in tempo and meter, and so generally the Dance Suite was formed. It included two types of dance: (1) the "basse danse" which was of an earthbound, slow, sombre and heavy nature, and its counterpart, (2) the "haute danse" which was lighter, higher, and faster. Common dance pairs were a slow, dignified *pavane* followed by a fast and spirited, triple time *galliard;* or the similar Italian rondo and *saltarello;* or the German *Tanz* and *Nach-Tanz.*

Gradually the composition of a Dance Suite became somewhat standardized so that the essentials included first the grave *allemande;* this was followed by a *courante* which is always an animated and lively dance; the third part of the suite was made up of the dignified, polished and courtly *sarabande;* the suite was then completed with the "hot and hasty" *gigue.* While this constituted the basic formula for a suite in the sixteenth and seventeenth centuries, it was stylish to inject another dance between the latter two required dances—a *minuet, bouree, polonaise, passepied, gavotte,* and so on—in the eighteenth century.

In addition to the accomplishments in secular music during the Renaissance (not only the dance suite, but songs, polyphonic ensemble works, and choral compositions), there were rich developments in the sacred music of the era. The Church services were most elaborate musically and employed the organ, choruses, and soloists. Altogether, the Renaissance was a music making age.

Of interest also to dancers was the beginning of the development of the *ground bass* (basso ostinato). In this form there is a constantly repeated figure in the bass and, over this and around this, composers constructed freely moving variations.

Composers of the Renaissance who are of special interest to dancers include Orlando di Lasso, Giovanni da Palestrina (considered one of the greatest musicians of all time), Cristobal Morales, Gabrieli, Orlando Gibbons, William Byrd, Jacobus Gallus.

THE BAROQUE PERIOD
(1600-1750)

The descriptive adjective common to all the art work of the period is "baroque," meaning grandiose, ornate, heavy and rich. While the arts were magnificent and extravagant, they were at the same time clear and purposeful with a distinct dramatic spirit. The best of the works did not even border on the rococo or pompous—they were truly products of grandeur. In music, this spirit manifests itself in large-scale efforts, and it is not surprising that it was at this point in history that the large vocal forms were created—the opera, oratorio, and cantata.

The opera developed from the music-drama which had emerged during the latter part of the preceding period, and it was usual to insert dances and decorative spectacles between the entr'actes. The dance suite continued to develop musically and to expand into larger forms. Dancers and choreographers often refer to the Renaissance-Baroque era as the Preclassic Period.

As has been mentioned previously, polyphony reached its height during the late baroque age with works of supreme musicianship and vividness of imagination. The culminating figures of the era were Bach and Händel, polyphony reaching unrivaled perfection in the Bach fugues.

It is profitable for dancers to become well acquainted with the works of some of the earlier composers of the period for their music is very conducive to formalized, stylized, and uncluttered types of choreographies. Several important composers of the period were William Byrd, Giovanni Pergolesi, Henry Purcell, Domenico Scarlatti, and Heinrich Schütz.

THE CLASSICAL PERIOD
(1750-1820)

During the end of the "Preclassic Period," or perhaps we should say at the beginning of the Classical Period, the Dance Suite as such faded as a dance endeavor and became more important as an independent musical undertaking. Two dances, the Pavane and the Galliard, disappeared altogether, and the Gavotte and Minuet were substituted. This was perhaps a highly significant substitution since these two dances exemplify the flavor of classicism in music—the grace, the formality, the decorativeness, and the extravagant development of melody. The classical spirit in the arts is epitomized by discipline and reserve, restraint and purity.

Somewhere, in between the Preclassic and Classical periods, the BALLET developed and came into its own in the luxurious court of Louis XIV, having been imported to France from Italy. While royalty sometimes participated in the ballet, dance no longer served only as a social function. It was again elevated into a position among the performing arts and became a means of expressing a dramatic idea. Dance artists were trained and ballet presentations were offered for aristocratic audiences. So great was the interest in ballet that efforts at initiating even a national opera were preceded by about ten years by a royal "Académie de Dance." Modern ballet really was inaugurated by Louis XIV with the founding in 1661 of "L'Académie Nationale de Musique et de la Danse."

Naturally, the musical composers of the period wholeheartedly embraced this new development. They wrote ballets per se, and a ballet was a welcome addition to any opera, a musical invention of about the same time.

The earliest surviving music directly written for ballet is the "Ballet Comique de la Reine" (1581). Lully is credited with introducing ballet into opera and, in fact, he with Molière created a combination play-ballet in which the ballet, rather than being a decorative adjunct, forwarded the action of the story ("Le Bourgeois Gentilhomme," 1670). The dancer-choreographer Noverre played a most prominent part in the development of the ballet and is known to have collaborated with the composers Gluck and Mozart.

One of the most important musical contributions of the Classical Period was the development of the Symphony.

Composers of the late Baroque and Classical Periods include Bach, Couperin, Gluck, Händel, Haydn, Mozart, and Rameau.

THE ROMANTIC PERIOD (1820-1900)

Bridging the Classical and Romantic Periods was Beethoven, the individualist, one of the greatest musical geniuses of all time. It is fascinating to watch the development which runs through his early works. They begin with the promise of much substance, yet these selections are fine examples of the grace and levity of the classical spirit. Gradually the compositions become more heroic, fuller in dynamics, darker in timbre, and truly monumental in scope.

The doors to Romanticism opened with the later Beethoven sonatas and symphonies, the latter of which climax with the famous Ninth. His one opera, "Fidelio," heralded the coming of a new era with the musical and literary dramatization of romantic love, heroism, freedom, love of country, and fidelity. The formalized and disciplined classicism thus gave way once more to the beginnings of self expression, fresh material, freedom of form, and romanticism.

During the nineteenth century the ballet began to enter into its most highly developed and elaborate sphere of existence. Composers after Beethoven all wrote lengthy and full scores, most of which have continued to be great orchestral favorites and mainstays of the ballet repertoire to this day. Some examples of these ballets which have come down to us directly from the nineteenth century scene include *Rosamunde* by Schubert; *Aurora's Wedding* and *Swan Lake* by Tschaikovsky; *Giselle* by Adolphe Adam; *Le Source* and *Coppelia* by Delibes; and music by Chopin which was arranged into a ballet called *Les Sylphides*.

Spectacle in the grand manner flourished in the nineteenth century romantic theater. Opera became "grand opera," and the ballets were truly grandiose as well. Scenery, costumes, and all theatrics were quite elaborate, and the defiance of gravity often went to the extent of having the dancers swing across the stage, suspended in mid-air by wires, in order to provide yet another romantic ingredient, that of the supernatural, the fairy tale quality.

The Romantic Period was an era of elegance. Music was enriched on all fronts. Melodies became fuller and were developed into less rigid phrases. Forms were expanded to include stylization of the most popular and traditional folk dances. Waltzes, polkas, and mazurkas were given elaborate treatment not only in the ballet scores which featured them almost exclusively, but also in the concert repertoire. One of these forms, the Austrian folk-waltz, the Laendler, received particular attention and emerged as the Viennese Waltz. It became a great favorite due to the genius of Johann Strauss who elevated it from the extended concert Laendler (step-hop waltz) of Joseph Lanner to a most sophisticated and truly elegant treatment which enabled it to flourish simultaneously in the grand ballroom, in the concert hall, and in the theater.

Orchestration also was expanded during the Romantic Period with a more extensive use being made of the brass, the woodwind, and the percussion sections. Vocal music reached an unsurpassed peak due to the very nature of romanticism. Nineteenth century lieder and chansons still are regarded as the epitome of vocal literature in the concert singer's repertoire. Dancers would be wise to probe occasionally into this field of vocal music, as well as into that of unscored poetry, for movement and choreographic stimuli.

Composers of the Romantic era include many of the immortal names in music, such as Beethoven, Brahms, Chopin, Donizetti, Fauré, Liszt, Moussorgsky, Mendelssohn, Schubert, Tschaikovsky, Wagner, Verdi, and many others.

THE TWENTIETH CENTURY (1900-   )

Radical and contradictory experimentation characterizes twentieth century musical undertakings. Composers have departed from the preceding romantic period in ways which may be classified into broad tendencies. Regardless of the three "isms" mentioned below, however, Schoenberg and Stravinsky are generally acknowledged as the leading pioneers in the important musical revolutions of our century.

Impressionism

Toward the end of the nineteenth and into the first part of the twentieth century, a new trend was apparent in all of the arts. Painters, poets, and composers, chiefly in France, explored new directions. Basically, the movement was a reaction and a protest against the massiveness and exuberance of Wagnerian music, against the complete and lush realism of painting, and against the dramatic and narrative excesses of romanticism in general.

Though impressionism has retained many aspects of romanticism, it deliberately strives for a vagueness and an elusiveness. Impressionists feel that suggestion and insinuation are stronger powers than realistic expression, and are less limiting. The French symbolist poet, Mallarmé, explained the movement in these words, "To name an object is to sacrifice three fourths of that enjoyment which comes from the pleasure of guessing bit by bit. To suggest, that is our dream."

Impressionists, therefore, turn away from the formal aspects of classicism and the personal feeling of romanticism and seek rather a feeling of liquidity and fluidity. The method is to hint, to intimate, to remind, and to allude. An emphasis is placed on light, both visual and audible. Through subtlety in sound and meaning, through an obscurity and a mistiness that has been described as a "luminous fog atmosphere," the impressionist seeks to stimulate the imagination.

The principal impressionistic composers include Debussy, Ravel, Roussel, and Satie in France; Delius in England; Scriabin in Russia; and Griffes in the United States.

Expressionism

A second direction which musical literature has taken during this century is described as Expressionism. This is another term that has been borrowed from the visual arts and signifies a subjective manifestation of the self which usually results in symbolization of thought, in abstractions, and ultimately in surrealism. Polytonality and atonality (explained in the following pages) are aspects of this trend in music. Expressionism evidences itself in a disregard for conventional solutions to problems of aesthetics, and takes great liberties in form, meter, and so on. The movement developed up to about 1930, mostly among German composers; it is, however, presently enjoying a vigorous universal revival.

The chief expressionistic composers include Alban Berg, Schoenberg, and Webern of the Viennese School; and Krenek, now in the United States.

Neoclassicism

Neoclassicism is the term given to the modern composer's tendency to return to the classic style.

Eighteenth century formal development is recalled, but while there is a return to contrapuntal disciplines and to clarity of expression, this is all wrought within the twentieth century idiom. A classic spirit prevails but the old classicism is not imitated.

Representative literature in the neoclassic vein has been written by the Russians, Prokofiev and Stravinsky, and by Hindemith in Germany.

SEQUENTIAL EVENTS IN MUSIC-DANCE HISTORY

Following is a chart which presents in outline form sequential events of importance in the history of music and dance. This outline is confined to a consideration of the development of these arts in our western civilization. It is presented as a study-aid only, as a broad contour map, the shadings of which may be filled in from time to time by the reader.

No attempt has been made to be inclusive, for individual works and composers are entirely too numerous to make a complete listing possible. We have attempted rather to picture the historical parallelism and continuity of music and dance and to show how these arts fit together. We have, of necessity, indicated developments of great consequence only, and historic landmarks have been noted merely by a word or two. Some choreographers and composers for dance who have been noted elsewhere in these pages are omitted from this outline, while other new names appear here.

An attempt has been made to choose significant works for inclusion, works which have contributed materially to the development of ballet and the modern dance, but we recognize that many have been omitted.

SEQUENTIAL EVENTS IN MUSIC – DANCE HISTORY

TIME	MUSICAL LANDMARKS	COMPOSERS	DANCE HIGHLIGHTS	CHOREOGRAPHERS (COMPOSERS)
800	*MONODY* Plainsong, Organum, Gregorian Chant	Troubadours Trouvères Minnesingers	Jongleurs Court Jesters *FOLK DANCE* (Throughout the centuries)	
MIDDLE AGES	EARLY POLYPHONY Ars Antiqua, Ars Nova Madrigal	Bertrand de Born Adam de la Halle Wolfram von Eschenbach		
1300	First Polyphonic Mass	Landino Machaut		
THE FIFTEENTH CENTURY	*POLYPHONY* *Music Notation* Rise of Keyboard instruments Lied, Chanson Mass, Passion	Dufay Ockeghem Josquin des Pres	Beginnings of *BALLET AMBULATOIRE* (a forerunner of classical ballet, said to have originated in Portugal; a processional pageant of mime and dance)	
THE SIXTEENTH CENTURY	Ricercar, Lute *Instrumental Music* Protestant Chorale Basse danse, Haute danse *Music Printing* Magnificat, Huguenot Psalter Virginalists	Lejeune Lasso Palestrina Gabrieli Byrd Morley Bull Galilei	*BALLET COMIQUE* (1580) "PRECLASSIC SUITE" Pavane, Gagliard, Allemade, Sarabande, Courante, Gigue	

THE RENAISSANCE

SEQUENTIAL EVENTS IN MUSIC – DANCE HISTORY

TIME	MUSICAL LANDMARKS	COMPOSERS	DANCE HIGHLIGHTS*		COMPOSER	DATE
THE BAROQUE PERIOD THE SEVENTEENTH CENTURY	*DANCE SUITE*	Frescobaldi	COURT MASQUES MIME			
	Divertissements (Concerts at the Court)					
	Arias Concerto Grosso	Couperin	Pavane, Galliard disappear; Menuet, Gavotte, Bourée added to Dance Suite			
	Cantata, Recitative	Corelli				
	Opera	Monteverdi	*BALLET DE COUR*			
	Toccata, Prelude, and Fugues		(Court ballet began at the celebration of the marriage of the eldest son of Catherine de Medici to Mary, Queen of Scots, April 24, 1558. Historical ballet begins 1580).			
	Oratorios	Lully				
		Rameau	**TITLE**	**CHOREOGRAPHER**		
	Orchestra		Ballet de la Nuit	Louis XIV danced the Sun King	Lully	1653
	Counterpoint	Vivaldi	Le Marriage Forcé	Pierre Beauchamp (Louis XIV, Lully, and Beauchamp dance)	Lully	1664
		Bach				
		Gluck				
		Händel				
THE CLASSIC PERIOD THE EIGHTEENTH CENTURY	*THE SONATA FORM*		*THE CLASSIC BALLET*			
			TITLE	**CHOREOGRAPHER**		
	Chamber ensemble	Haydn	Les Indes Galantes	L. Fuzeliev	Rameau	1735
			Don Juan	G. Angiolini	Gluck	1761
	Symphony		Les Petits Riens	J. G. Noverre	Mozart	1778
			Iphigenia in Tauris	J. G. Noverre	Gluck	1779
	Opera buffa	Mozart	La Fille Mal Gardée	C. Didelot	Bossi	1786
		Beethoven				

*We are indebted to John Dougherty, staff correspondent for *Dance Magazine* for assistance in compiling information on the historical development of the ballet.

50

SEQUENTIAL EVENTS IN MUSIC – DANCE HISTORY

TIME	MUSICAL LANDMARKS	COMPOSERS	DANCE HIGHLIGHTS		COMPOSER	DATE
			THE ROMANTIC BALLET			
			TITLE	CHOREOGRAPHER		
THE NINETEENTH CENTURY (THE ROMANTIC ERA)	The Romantic Sonata	Beethoven	The Waltz, Mazurka, Schottische, Polonaise in the ballrooms			
		Schubert				
	SYMPHONIES · Grand Opera	Schumann				
		Wagner				
	Solo Concerto	Brahms				
		Donizetti	The Creatures of Prometheus	S. Vigano	Beethoven	1801
	Art Songs	Verdi				
	Ballet Music	Mendelssohn	La Sylphide	F. Taglioni	Schnitzhoeffer	1832
		Gounod	Giselle	J. Coralli-J. Perrot	Adam	1841
	Symphonic Poem	Rimsky-Korsakoff	Le Jugement de Paris	J. Perrot	Pugni	1846
		Chopin	Genna	F. Cerito	Gabrielli	1854
	The Piano Virtuoso	Liszt	Don Quichotte	M. Petipa	Minkus	1869
		Franck	Coppelia	A. Saint-Leon	Delibes	1870
		Tschaikowsky	Sylvia	L. Merante	Delibes	1876
	Nationalism					
	The "Salons"	Delibes	The Sleeping Beauty	M. Petipa	Tschaikowsky	1890
	The Waltz	Johann Strauss	The Nutcracker	L. Ivanov	Tschaikowsky	1892
		Grieg				
	Operetta	Richard Strauss	Swan Lake	M. Petipa-L. Ivanov	Tschaikowsky	1895
		Sibelius				

SEQUENTIAL EVENTS IN MUSIC – DANCE HISTORY

TIME	MUSICAL LANDMARKS	COMPOSERS	DANCE HIGHLIGHTS		COMPOSER	DATE
			THE DIAGHILEFF BALLET (exerpts)			
			TITLE	**CHOREOGRAPHER**		
		Mahler				
		Puccini	Les Sylphides	M. Fokine	Chopin (orch. Glazunov)	1908
THE	Late Romanticism		Prince Igor	M. Fokine	Borodin	1909
		Rachmaninoff	Le Carnaval	M. Fokine	Schumann	1910
			Firebird	M. Fokine	Stravinsky	1910
			Petrouchka	M. Fokine	Stravinsky	1911
		Sibelius	Afternoon of a Faun	V. Nijinsky	Debussy	1912
			Rites of Spring	V. Nijinsky	Stravinsky	1913
TWENTIETH		Richard Strauss	La Boutique Fantasque	L. Massine	Rossini-Respighi	1919
			Three Cornered Hat	L. Massine	de Falla	1919
			Apollon Musagete	G. Balanchine	Stravinsky	1928
			The Prodigal Son	G. Balanchine	Prokofiev	1929
			Le Bal	G. Balanchine	Rieti	1929
			ISADORA DUNCAN			
CENTURY	Impressionism	Debussy	Revolutionary Etude	I. Duncan	Chopin	1900 ?
			Marseillaise		Chopin	1900 ?
		Delibes	Many semi-improvised works to music by Beethoven, Wagner, Schubert, Gluck, Bach, Tschaikowsky			
			DENISHAWN			
		Ravel	Rahda	R. St. Denis	Arrangement of East Indian music	1906
			Cobra	R. St. Denis		
		Roussel	Yogi	R. St. Denis		
			White Jade	R. St. Denis		
		Satie	Xochitel	T. Shawn	Grunn	1920
			Orpheus	T. Shawn	Gluck	1930
			MARY WIGMAN			
			Face of the Night	M. Wigman	Percussion, flute, etc.	
			Witch Dance	M. Wigman		
			Lament	M. Wigman		

SEQUENTIAL EVENTS IN MUSIC – DANCE HISTORY

TIME	MUSICAL LANDMARKS	COMPOSERS	DANCE HIGHLIGHTS		COMPOSER	DATE
			MUSICAL COMEDY Some important choreographies			
			TITLE	CHOREOGRAPHER		
THE TWENTIETH CENTURY (cont.)	Jazz Musical Comedy	Bernstein Cole Ellington Gershwin Loewe Rodgers	Allegro	Agnes de Mille	Rodgers	1947
			Annie Get Your Gun	Helen Tamiris	Berlin	1946
			Bloomer Girl	Agnes de Mille	Arlen	1944
			Brigadoon	Agnes de Mille	Loewe	1947
			Carousel	Agnes de Mille	Rodgers	1945
			Fancy Free	Jerome Robbins	Bernstein	1944
			Finian's Rainbow	Michael Kidd	Lane	1947
			Guys and Dolls	Michael Kidd	Loesser	1950
			Kiss Me Kate	Hanya Holm	Porter	1948
			My Fair Lady	Hanya Holm	Loewe	1956
			Oklahoma!	Agnes de Mille	Rodgers	1943
			On the Town	Jerome Robbins	Bernstein	1944
			Redhead	Bob Fosse	Hague	1958
			The King and I	Jerome Robbins	Rodgers	1951
			West Side Story	Jerome Robbins	Bernstein	1957

Chapter 11

MODERN MUSIC

During the first half of the twentieth century all of the arts departed radically from tradition. The first World War no doubt accelerated and sharpened the breach with the past, and subsequent world events have added increasing restlessness and uncertainty, violence and strife. There remains no guiding tradition. Virtual negation of time and distance has resulted in a blending of cultures. We live in an era of tremendous speed, of discovery, of complexity, of experimentation and invention, and of fear. It is not surprising that there has been a revolution in all artistic endeavors.

Modern music is a blend of many aspects of that which is "modern" in other artistic fields, and all are mirrors of an apprehensive society. Music has gone off on various tangents—it has been energetic, insecure, and unconventional in these directions and in its experiments. It is astonishing that the results are as positive and not as confusing as one might have expected.

DEVELOPMENT OF THE MODERN STYLE

Twentieth century music has been marked by technical developments and fundamental changes, and it is these aspects which distinguish it. These alterations, however, make modern music bewildering and sometimes even unintelligible. New concepts of tonality have developed, and new emphases have been placed on harmony, tone color, rhythm, and melody.

Tonality

Since the time of Bach, music has been developed around an accepted sense of tonality. This involves the principle of a "key" in music. A "key" gives a composition a certain character because the notes which make up the tonal system have a long-accepted family relationship. Modulations (transitions) made to other keys add interest and new points of view, but traditionally these were made to a set of accepted tonal relationships. The foundations of the prevailing system were the major and minor scales, and the combination of different tones built from them.

In modern music, modulation is less regularly employed, and related and unrelated keys are often placed next to each other (*Multitonality*). In extreme cases, two or more keys may appear simultaneously within a passage or throughout a whole work. This simultaneous use of tonalities (*Polytonality*) results in an unconventional and, therefore, disquieting group of sounds. It is only one step farther, of course, to a complete lack of adherence to any key at all. The latter (*Atonality*) results in an extreme use of dissonance and an outright abolition of the classical system.

Dissonance, which has always existed as a tension provoker in music, has been employed increasingly from the time of Wagner through the Impressionists. Stravinsky and Schoenberg individually made revolutionary breaks with the past in this respect. In addition to the innovations in tonality, this century has seen a return of the early church modes and proposals of other modal systems (that is, other fixed schemes). All of this has resulted in new, unusual harmony which has been met both with enthusiasm and hostility.

Harmony

Modern harmonies are a blend of consonances and dissonances. Consonances are conventional intervals and harmonic units which result in a pleasing agreement of simultaneously produced sounds. Dissonances, on the other hand, are chords which, because of their defiance of accepted rules, pose tension and stress. Dissonances sometimes outnumber the consonances in a modern work.

The most conspicuous musical experiments have taken place in the realm of harmony, and the accepted theories have been challenged with new proposals. Experiments have been carried out changing the customary progression of half and whole steps, thus releasing the composer from the order of the major and minor scales. The resulting "Twelve Tone System" gives equal weight to each of the twelve half steps of the octave and, therefore, alters the traditional relationship between the notes in the scale. (In our chromatic scale there is an established relationship between every sound and the Tonic, or first note of the scale. This association does not exist in the Twelve-Tone System.)

The pentatonic scales of some Oriental civilizations and the quarter tones of the Hindu and other musical cultures also have been introduced to our Western world. All of these harmonic resources have been incorporated into our own creative efforts.

Timbre

Not only have tonalities and harmonies been affected, but also timbre or tone color. A considerable amount of experimentation has been taking place in the field of new instruments. Electronic sounds are utilized, old instruments are played in new ways, and recording equipment, especially the magnetic tape, has become an ingenious "instrument" for producing music as well as a means of preserving sound. The juxta-position of sounds and passages, and the extremes in slowing down or speeding up of tempi (only possible with electronic manipulation), have resulted in some very interesting, if inconclusive and not yet clearly directed results.

Rhythm

Perhaps the most intriguing innovation to the dancer is the new use of rhythm in modern music. There has been a general letting down of traditional barriers and, as a result, a greater elasticity and variety in the use of metric structures. The rhythmical system is now less symmetrical. While 2/4, 3/4, 4/4, and 6/8 times still predominate, 5/4, and 7/4, and 10/8, and other signatures have been introduced and found most interesting, mainly because of the absence of a recurring, predictable secondary accent within the measure.

Various rhythms following one another in rapid sequences such as 3/4, 2/4, 5/4, 2/4 and so on (*Mixed Meter*), and even *polyrhythms* are employed. The latter device, the playing of two different rhythms simul-taneously, is known as "Resultant Rhythm" in the dance terminology.

The shifting or displacing of accents to ordinarily weak beats produces syncopation, and this practice currently is used more freely and steadily than ever before in Western music.

Melody

Melody, too, has undergone drastic changes, and the contempory use of the melodic line is often even more startling and disquieting to the listener than harmonic dissonances. Melodies in the modern idiom do not invariably find a resting place or an anchorage spot, as has long been customary. We have always found pleasing the predictability of the flowing and ending of passages. Instead, melodies now are often left suspended, or else they skip about in unusual intervals. As a consequence, modern music is difficult

to "hum," and this, of course, is a bit unnerving to the uninitiated.

COMPOSERS OF THE TWENTIETH CENTURY

Musical techniques have been vastly extended by modern composers. The changes have not always been received with enthusiasm, but there are, nevertheless, a great number of contemporary compositions which are a piquant and satisfying blend of the past and present. The best of these works combine interesting new ideas with the particular and personal stamp of individual composers.

The following list of modern composers is far from complete. It seems appropriate, however, for dancers to be acquainted with some of the musicians who are the leaders in the trends which have developed during this century.

Debussy and Ravel are associated by everyone with *impressionistic* music; other composers who write in this vein include Roussel (France); Delius (England); de Falla and Albeniz (Spain); and Griffes (United States).

Schoenberg was the inventor of the Twelve Tone System. His Austrian-German followers are known as the "Viennese School." These *expressionistic* composers all employ radical atonality and dissonance: Berg, Krenek, and Webern.

Some of the principal leaders of the *neoclassic* in modern music are Hindemith, Prokofiev, and Stravinsky. Others who write with formal clarity and objectiveness include Antheil, Bartok, Casella, and Shostakovitch.

Other prominent contemporary composers, whose output has been high in quality and whose approach and style are recommended to dancers, include Bloch, Chavez, Dallapicolla, Eck, Honegger, Khatchaturian, Milhaud, Nono, Poulenc, Rebikov, Robles, Toch, Weill, and Villa-Lobos.

Attention should be directed especially to the number of composers in England and the United States. There are now, contrary to some periods in the past, a very significant list of writers in these countries who are making most important contributions to modern music. Dancers are encouraged to refer to the works of England's Benjamin, Berkeley, Bliss, Britten, Howells, Walton, and Vaughn Williams.

An obviously incomplete list of the many talented composers who write in the modern idiom in the United States includes Bernstein, Cage, Copland, Cowell, Dello Joio, Foss, Gillis, Harris, Nordoff, North, Persichetti, Piston, Riegger, William Schuman, Virgil Thomson, and Edgar Varèse.

There is a completely new trend in music, an out-growth of the Twelve Tone System, which involves the so-called "serial principle." It requires a controlled diversification of themes in relation not only to melody and counterpoint but, in addition, to rhythm. This method is a very experimental, intellectually conceived approach to composition. While it strictly follows rules set up by the composer, recognizable repetition of melodic themes is difficult to perceive. There is carefully planned manipulation of the same material but the result deliberately sounds like organized chaos. It is, however, interesting and provocative and often provides quite good music for the present trends in dance.

Some of the serial composers, by experimenting with wave lengths and frequencies, arrive at electronic music conceived by the same technique. Composition produced with electronic dials and circuits allows composers to organize sound and to extend its range in many ways otherwise impossible when using conventional musical sources. It also makes possible the use of new sources of sound for serious musical composition beyond those attainable with conventional musical instruments. In addition, rhythms and variations which are humanly not performable, and which therefore provide new emotional effects, may be produced. This new music naturally demands new types of notation. Instead of referring to notes such as E sharp or G flat, the composer may refer to sounds determined by an oscillator; the notes then have a frequency number such as "note 186."

Pierre Boulez, a French composer, is a recognized exponent of the serial technique. Another pioneer, Karlheinz Stockhausen, from Germany, in addition to employing the serial principle and composing in the traditional manner, also composes with electronic sounds. Furthermore, he writes compositions which leave aspects of the performance open to the interpreter. This is done by putting the composition into a pictorial design (e.g., an octagon) instead of in the traditional left-right horizontal line sequence. The performer can then elect to play the composition in terms of the design without following the customarily prescribed order of beginning, middle, and end. Other composers who are experimenting with new sources and uses or some include Edgar Varèse, and the Columbia University collaborators, Otto Luening and Vladimir Ussachevsky.

Since we are so accustomed to music composed and produced in the traditional idiom, it is natural that such innovations as those described above are being met with more criticism than popular enthusiasm. It is well to remember however, that historically, as each new musical innovation was introduced, it was censured, that the avant-garde has seldom found immediate popularity. Not even the composers who are attracted to these new media predict that electronic music will ever supplant the conventional variety; they simply are attempting to extend the boundaries of that which has heretofore been musically possible and are employing instruments previously used for reproduction (tape recorder, loudspeaker, radio), for production. Dancers should at least be aware of these musical innovations; they may find them the stimulus for interesting movement experimentations and sometimes fresh sources of accompaniment.

Chapter 12

CONTEMPORARY COMPOSERS FOR DANCE

Dance has always played an important part in stimulating musical composition. All composers have written for dance, either directly or indirectly, consciously or unconsciously. A list of any writer's works almost always includes ballets, compositions entitled "dances", arrangements in dance form, or entr'actes prepared for plays or operas. On the other hand, the fact that a composer has not worked directly with dancers, or has not been commissioned to produce a specific work for dance, need not influence the choreographer who is looking for material. The reader will find in the resource section of this book and throughout these pages, that works of such composers as Bartok, Prokofiev, Shostakovitch, and Satie are recommended highly. As far as we know, however, these composers while they have written ballet scores, have seldom worked directly with choreographers.

In the present chapter are cited some modern composers with whom we feel all students of dance literature should most certainly be acquainted because they have written *directly* and explicitly for dance, both modern and ballet.

COMPOSERS FOR DANCE

It is not only impossible to list all composers who have written directly for dance, but impractical to attempt an ennumeration of all the dance works of a given composer. Here then, in alphabetical order, is a *selected* group of contemporary composers, a sample of their dance literature, and the choreographer for whom each work was produced. These composers have thus had direct contact with the dance as collaborators with choreographers.

George Antheil

American Seranade.....................................Martha Graham
Course...Martha Graham
Dreams..George Balanchine

(His "Ballet Mecanique", a revolutionary work, has intrigued many dancers, but since it is definitely a "dance image", it usually defies visual comment. In this composition, Antheil employed mechanical pianos and electrical devices. In general, his works show neoclassical trends.)

Lennox Berkeley

The Judgment of Paris.........................Ninette de Valois

Leonard Bernstein

Facsimile...Jerome Robbins
Fancy Free...Jerome Robbins
(This well known composer has been very successful in many media: conducting, lecturing, composing, and concertizing. He has written musical comedy, ballet and opera as well as chamber music, orchestral and choral works.)

Arthur Bliss

Checkmate..Ninette de Valois
Miracle in the Gorbals..........................Robert Helpman

Henry Brant

City Portrait..Eugene Loring
Conflict...Helen Tamiris
Light...Helen Tamiris
The Great American Goof.........................Eugene Loring

John Cage

Antic Meet...Merce Cunningham
A Suite of Four Dancers.............................Hanya Holm
Ophelia...Jean Erdman
(Mr. Cage is music director and composer for Merce Cunningham. He is well known for his compositions for percussion orchestra and for the "prepared piano." He has introduced interesting and provocative ideas in tone color and form.)

Henry Leland Clarke
Sarabande for the Living..................................Jose Limon
Sarabande for the Dead..................................Jose Limon

Marius Constant
Contre-Pointe...Roland Petit

Aaron Copland
Appalachian Spring.....................................Martha Graham
Billy the Kid...Eugene Loring
Day on Earth...Doris Humphrey
Hear Ye Hear Ye..Ruth Page
Olympus Americanus..................................Helen Tamiris
Rodeo..Agnes de Mille

(Aaron Copland's "Music for the Theatre" and "El Salon Mexico" have been favorites of dancers and choreographers for many years. In fact, he has been one of the most active of all modern composers for dance and for the theatre. In addition, he has contributed magazine articles and has written at least two books, *What to Listen for in Music* and *Our New Music*.)

Henry Cowell
Dance of Introduction..................................Hanya Holm
Deep Song...Martha Graham
Immediate Tragedy.....................................Martha Graham

(Mr. Cowell is credited with pioneering in musical texture. Many of his compositions are for percussion and for the piano as a percussion instrument. The term "tone cluster" is his invention; it refers to the simultaneous playing of several notes either with the whole hand or the forearm to achieve a multiple, bunched sound. He has also experimented with other methods of playing the piano, including plucking and stroking the strings. John Cage and Roy Harris are often referred to as belonging to the "Cowell School" of composition.)

Norman Dello Joio
Diversion of Angels.....................................Martha Graham
On Stage..Michael Kidd
Prairie...Eugene Loring

Lehman Engel
Transitions...Martha Graham

Lukas Foss
Fantastic Dance...Nimura
Gift of the Magi..Simon Senenoff
The Heart Remembers...........................Doris Humphrey,
Charles Weidman
Within These Walls..................................Virginia Johnson

Ray Green
American Document....................................Martha Graham
Dance Sonata...May O'Donnell

Roy Harris
From This Earth..Hanya Holm
Song of the West......................................Doris Humphrey

(Many of Mr. Harris' scores have been used by foremost modern dancers. His compositions lend themselves beautifully to choreographic efforts.)

Lou Harrison
Conquest...Jean Erdman
Creature on a Journey................................Jean Erdman
Something to Please Everybody.................Jean Erdman

(Mr. Harrison's works provide rich material for the choreographer. His music is interesting in texture and offers a great variety in timbre and form. He has been active as a dancer and choreographer as well as a composer.)

Hans Hasting
Dance of Women..Mary Wigman
Sacrifice..Mary Wigman
Shifting Landscape.....................................Mary Wigman

Eugene Hemmer
Absynthe..Pola Nirenska
Legendary Forest.......................................May O'Donnel
Second Dance Concerto............................May O'Donnel
Somewhere Else Instead............................Beth Osgood

(Mr. Hemmer's Dance Sonata and Dance Concerto ideas are particularly interesting. These compositions use the solo dancer as an instrument; that is, the dancer plays the same role that a solo violin or piano plays in a concerto.)

Paul Hindemith
Herodiade..Martha Graham
The Four Temperaments...................George Balanchine

(This distinguished composer is largely responsible for neoclassical trends in modern music. His works are completely contemporary in feeling and are noted for the quality of the melodic line.)

David Holden
We, the Women.............................Gertrude Lippincott

Louis Horst
Act of Judgment...Martha Graham
Act of Piety..Martha Graham
El Penitente..Martha Graham
Frontier..Martha Graham
Primitive Mysteries...................................Martha Graham

(Mr. Horst is recognized, probably unanimously, as the dean of modern dance music. He has been the mentor, composer, and accompanist for leading dancers, and has been revered and feared by aspiring ones. His classes in choreography, music for dance, and particularly his courses in the "Pre-Classics", have been considered essential in the education of the modern dancer. He is the founder of the *Dance Observer*, a monthly publication which enjoys a wide circulation among many dance enthusiasts, and is the author of the book, *Pre-Classic Dance Forms*.)

Maurice Jacobson

David.................................Alicia Markova, Anton Dolin

Hunter Johnson

Deaths and Entrances...............................Martha Graham
Letter to the World...................................Martha Graham

Norman Lloyd

Dance of Work and Play............................Hanya Holm
Inquest...Doris Humphrey
Lament for Ignacio Sanchez Mejias........Doris Humphrey
Panorama..Martha Graham
Quest...Charles Weidman
Tabloid...Charles Weidman

(Mr. Lloyd, like Mr. Horst, is a well known dance critic, an authority on music for the dance, and an esteemed composer for choreographers.)

Freda Miller

Fables of Our Time...............................Charles Weidman
Windows...Hanya Holm

Paul Nordoff

Every Soul Is a Circus..........................Martha Graham
Salem Shore..Martha Graham
Tallyho...Agnes de Mille

Lionel Nowak

Danzas Mexicanas...Jose Limon
On My Mother's Side............................Charles Weidman
Square Dances........Doris Humphrey, Charles Weidman
The Green Land......................................Doris Humphrey
The Wages of Sin..................................Charles Weidman

(Mr. Nowak has been particularly interested in music for the modern dance and has produced scores for leading dancers. He was an accompanist-composer for the Humphrey-Weidman Dance Company for some years.)

Genevieve Pitot

Liberty Song..Helen Tamaris
Roads to Hell...Eleanor King

Wallingford Riegger

New Dance...Doris Humphrey
Theatre Piece..Doris Humphrey
Trend..Hanya Holm
With My Red Fires..................................Doris Humphrey

William Schuman

Night Journey..Martha Graham
Undertow..Anthony Tudor

Igor Stravinsky

Agon...George Balanchine
Appolo...Michael Fokine
Dances Concertantes............................George Balanchine
Jeu de Cartes...George Balanchine
Petrouchka...Michael Fokine
The Firebird...Michael Fokine

(Although Stravinsky undoubtedly would have become recognized for his genius without any of his numerous and brilliant ballet scores, it is the opinion of many that his association with Diaghilev hastened the coming of his fame.)

Virgil Thomson

Filling Station..Lou Christensen

(Mr. Thomson's scores have held great appeal for dancers. His various musical "Portraits" and also the "Louisiana Story" are very performable works.)

Other Composers for Dance

Some other composers who have collaborated with choreographers include Norman Cazden (New Dance Group); Herbert Ellwell (Dance Repertory Theatre); Herbert Haufrecht (Charles Weidman); Harrison Kerr (Bennington School of the Dance); Ernest Lubin (Martha Graham); Morris Mamorsky (Humphrey-Weidman Dance Company); Gian-Carlo Menotti (Ballet International); Nicholas Nabokoff (Ballet Russe de Monte Carlo); Alex North (Anna Sokolow Dance Company).

Resource Center

Attention is directed to the American Music Center (250 West 57th Street, New York 19, New York), a nonprofit institution for composers, conductors, publishers, and choreographers. Information about contemporary American music and composers may be secured by writing to the center. American music has been assembled here for reference and study, and the center provides many services and facilities that will be of use to accompanists, dance teachers and choreographers.

DANCE ACCOMPANIST-COMPOSERS

One final group of musicians deserve special mention, the dance specialists. These are people who have concentrated virtually exclusively for a number of years on music for the dance, or who have made dance accompaniment a life's profession. They have worked as accompanists, composers, music-resource persons, and dance-music publishers. Among the accompanist-teacher-composers across the country who have devoted themselves almost entirely to this field at one time or another are John Cooper, Ted Courtney, Lucia Dlugoszewski, Julian Erbaz, Shirley Genther, Pia Gilbert, Ralph Gilbert, Joseph Harwes, Eugene Hemmer, Louis Horst, Clarence Jackson, Daniel Jahn, Hazel Johnson, Ben Johnsten, Ulrich Kessler, Eugene Lester, Evelyn Lohoeffer, Norman Lloyd, Ruth Lloyd, William Malm, Stephan McDermott, Jess Meeker, Freda Miller, Cameron McCosh, Duncan Pierce, Genevieve Pitot, Trudi Rittman, Gertrude Robinson, Charles Rybaki, David Tudor, and John Wilson.

Collectively, the accompanist-composers listed above have worked in many educational institutions and professional studios, including the following: Connecticut College, Stephens College, University of California at Berkeley, University of California at Los Angeles, University of Cincinnati, University of Illinois, University of Southern California, University of Wisconsin, Unversity of Nebraska, and Wayne University. The same group of musicians includes accompanist-composers who have been associated with individual choreographers and dance groups: The Dance Quartet, Margaret Dietz, Martha Graham, Erick Hawkins, Doris Humphrey and Charles Weidman, Agnes de Mille, The New Dance Group, Steffi Nossen, Sark Studio, Sybil Shearer, Paul Taylor, and Mary Wigman.

Chapter 13

PIANO WORKS

The following list of piano works is offered as a guide to the accompanist. We suggest that he browse through the material at the local music library and music stores. The pieces were chosen with regard to their suitability for dance composition.

Special attention is called to the new publishing company, Orchesis Publications, 200 West 57th Street, New York, which publishes "CHOREOMUSIC," music written for dance by dance composers.

(MS) stands for "Manuscript Copy" and indicates that while the compositions are not yet published, they are available from the composers for a very reasonable fee, usually at production cost.

Music Specially Selected for Modern Dance

Bach, Johann Sebastian. *A Collection of Twenty-One Pieces.* New York: G. Schirmer Inc.

Bach, Johann Sebastian. *The Well Tempered Clavichord.* New York: Kalmus.

Bach, Johann Sebastian. *English Suites.* New York: G. Schirmer Inc.

Bach, Johann Sebastian. *French Suites.* New York: G. Schirmer Inc.

Bach, Johann Sebastian. *Partitas.* New York: G. Schirmer Inc.

Bach, Johann Sebastian. *Italian Concerts.* Edition No. 4484. New York: Peters.

Bach, Johann Sebastian. *Inventions.* New York: Kalmus Piano Series, or Shirmer's Library of Musical Classics.

Barber, Samuel. *Excursions.* New York: G. Schirmer Inc.

Bartok, Bela. *For Children.* New York: Boosey and Hawkes Inc.

Bartok, Bela. *Allegro Barbaro.* New York: Boosey and Hawkes Inc.

Bartok, Bela. *Nine Little Pieces.* New York: Boosey and Hawkes Inc.

Bartok, Bela. *Mikrokosmos,* 6 volumes. New York: Boosey and Hawkes Inc.

Bartok, Bela. *Out of Doors Suite.* New York: Boosey and Hawkes Inc.

Bartok, Bela. *Piano Selections.* New York: G. Schirmer Inc.

Bartok, Bela. *Three Rondos On Folk Tunes.* New York: Boosey and Hawkes Inc.

Beethoven, Ludwig van. *Bagatelles.* New York: International Music Co.

Beethoven, Ludwig van. *Eccossaises.* New York: Harbin Baltic Co.

Beethoven, Ludwig van. *Piano Works* (Bagatelles, Polonaises, Rondos, etc.). New York: Peters.

Bowles, Paul. *Folk Preludes.* New York: Mercury Music Corp.

Bowles, Paul. *Six Preludes.* New York: New York Music Press.

Brahms, Johannes. *Waltzes.* New York: G. Schirmer Inc.

Casella, Alfred. *Pezzi Infantili.* Universal Edition. New York: Associated Music Publishers.

Castelnuovo, Tedesco Mario. *Six Pieces In Form Of Canons.* New York: Ricordi and Co.

Chavez, Carlos. *Ten Preludes.* New York: G. Schirmer Inc.

Chopin, Frederic. *Mazurkas.* C. F. Peter Edition. New York: G. Schirmer Inc.

Chopin, Frederic. *Preludes.* New York: G. Schirmer Inc.

Chopin, Frederic. *Waltzes.* Universal Edition. New York: Associated Music Publishers, Inc.

Clarke, Henry Leland. *Six Characters For Piano.* New York: American Composers Alliance.

Copland, Aaron. *Four Piano Blues.* New York: Boosey and Hawkes Inc.

Cowell, Henry. *Celtic Set.* New York: G. Schirmer Inc.

Cowell, Henry. *The Irishman Dances.* New York: Carl Fischer.

Creston, Paul. *Six Preludes For Piano.* New York: Leeds Music Corp.

Debussy, Claude. *Pour le Piano.* New York: International Music Co.

Debussy, Claude. *Preludes,* Books I and II. Paris: Durand et fils.

Debussy, Claude. *Children's Corner.* Paris: Durand et fils.

Dello Joio, Norman. *Preludes: To A Young Dancer, To A Young Musician.* New York: G. Schirmer Inc.

Feldman, Morton. *Illusions For Piano.* New York: New Music Edition. New Music, Vol. 23, no. 4, July 1950.

Freed, Isadore. *Caprice.* Philadelphia: Elkan-Vogel.

Gershwin, George. *Preludes.* New York: New World Music Corp.

Harris, Roy. *Ten American Ballads.* New York: Carl Fischer.

Hemmer, Eugene. *Two Alsatian Dances.* (MS). New York: American Music Center, 250 W 57.

Hemmer, Eugene. *American Miniatures.* (MS). New York: American Music Center, 250 W 57.

Hemmer, Eugene. *Four Impromptus.* (MS). New York: American Music Center, 250 W 57.

Hindemith, Paul. *Kaviermusik.* London: Schott and Co., Ltd.

Hindemith, Paul. *Tanzstuecke.* London: Schott and Co., Ltd.

Honegger, Arthur. *Sept Pieces Breves.* Paris: La Sirene Musicale.

Kabalevski, Dmitri. *Four Preludes.* New York: Leeds Co.

Kanitz, Ernst. *Magic Dance.* (MS). Van Nuys, California: Ernst Kanitz, 6206 Murietta.

Kanitz, Ernst. *Solemn Dance.* (MS). Van Nuys, California: Ernst Kanitz, 6206 Murietta.

Kanitz, Ernst. *Five Dances.* (MS). Van Nuys, California: Ernst Kanitz, 6206 Murietta.

Kremenliev, Boris. *Six Miniatures.* New York: Leeds Co.

Kremenliev, Boris. *Three Preludes.* (MS). Los Angeles: U.C.L.A. Music Building.

Krenek, Ernst. *Little Suite.* New York: Associated Music Publishers, Inc.

Krenek, Ernst. *Twelve Short Piano Pieces.* New York: G. Schirmer Inc.

Krenek, Ernst. *Eight Piano Pieces.* New York: Music Press Inc.

Kubik, Gail. *Dance Soliloquy.* New York: Mercury Music Corp.

Lackner, Stephan. *Nostalgic Suite.* (MS). Santa Barbara, California: Stephan Lackner, 601 El Bosque Road.

Luening, Otto. *Two Inventions.* New York: Mercury Music Corp.

Milhaud, Darius. *L'Enfant Aime.* New York: Leeds Music Corp.

Milhaud, Darius. *Four Sketches.* New York: Mercury Music Corp.

Milhaud, Darius. *Saudados de Brazil.* London: Schott and Co., Ltd.

Persichetti, Vincent. *Little Piano Book.* Philadelphia: Elkan-Vogel.

Persichetti, Vincent. *Parades For Piano.* Philadelphia: Elkan-Vogel.

Pinto, Octavio. *Childrens Festival.* New York: G. Schirmer Inc.

Pinto, Octavio. *Little Suite.* New York: G. Schirmer Inc.

Pisk, Paul. *Engine Room, A Motor Study For Piano.* New York: Leeds Co.

Poulenc, Francis. *Mouvements Perpetuels.* London: Chester.

Prokoffiev, Serge. *Music For Children.* New York: G. Schirmer Inc.

Prokoffiev, Serge. *Album Of Piano Pieces.* New York: Edward B. Marks Corp.

Ravel, Maurice. *Album Of Masterpieces.* New York: Edward B. Marks Corp.

Ravel, Maurice. *Le Tombeau de Couperin.* Paris: Durand et fils.

Riegger, Wallingford. *New And Old—Twelve Pieces For Piano.* New York: Boosey and Hawkes Inc.

Satie, Erik. *Gymnopedies.* Paris: Rouart, Lerolle et Co., and New York: Edward B. Marks Corp.

Scarlatti, Domenico. *Sonatas.* New York: Ricordi and Co.

Schoenberg, Arnold. *Kavierstuecke,* op. 11. Universal edition. New York: Associated Music Publishers.

Schoenberg, Arnold. *Six Little Piano Pieces,* op. 19. New York: Associated Music Publishers.

Schoenberg, Arnold. *Fünf Klavierstuecke.* New York: Associated Music Publishers.

Schoenberg, Arnold. *Suite For Piano.* Universal Edition New York: Associated Music Publishers.

Schubert, Franz. *Waltzes.* New York: G. Schirmer Inc.

Schumann, Robert. *Album For The Young.* New York: G. Schirmer Inc.

Schumann, Robert. *Scenes From Childhood.* New York: G. Schirmer Inc.

Shostakovich, Dmitri. *Preludes.* New York: International Music Co.

Shostakovich, Dmitri. *Fantastic Dances.* New York: International Music Co.

Shostakovich, Dmitri. *Polka.* New York: International Music Co.

Smit, Leo. *Rural Elegy.* New York: Boosey and Hawkes Inc.

Stravinsky, Igor. *Circus Polka.* New York: Associated Music Publishers.

Stravinsky, Igor. *Album Of Masterpieces.* New York: Edward B. Marks Corp.

Thomson, Virgil. *Ten Etudes.* New York: Carl Fischer.

Thomson, Virgil. *Five Two-Part Inventions.* Philadelphia: Elkan-Vogel.

Toch, Ernst. *Ideas.* Los Angeles: Delkas.

Villa-Lobos, Heitor. *As Tres Marias.* New York: Carl Fischer.

Villa-Lobos, Heitor. *The Baby's Family.* New York: Edward B. Marks Corp.

Webern, Anton von. *Variations For Piano.* Universal Edition. New York: Associated Music Publishers.

Tsherepnin, Alexander. *Bagatelles.* New York: International Music Co.

Collections Specially Chosen for Modern Dance

Abrams, Esther. *Meet Modern Music.* (Original piano music; simple to play). New York: Mercury Music Corp.

Album Des Six. (Compositions by Auric, Durey, Honegger, Milhaud, Poulenc, Tailleferre). Paris: Max Eschig.

Collection Moderne. (Piano pieces by contemporary composers). New York: Edward B. Marks Corp.

Early Keyboard Music. Vol. I Byrd to Scarlatti, Vol. II. Couperin to Rameau. New York: G. Schirmer Inc.

Fifty One Piano Pieces From The Modern Repertoire. New York: G. Schirmer Inc.

Klavierbuch (Modern Works). Universal Edition. New York: Associated Music Publishers.

Musik Aus Alter Zeit (Music of Ancient Times). Vol. I Pre Bach, Vol. II Bach and Handel. Cologne: Arno.

Musik Der Zeit. Universal Edition. New York: Associated Music Publishers.

Musik Fur Taenzer. Universal Edition. New York: Associated Music Publishers.

Music Specifically Composed for Modern Dance

Hemmer, Eugene. *American Miniatures,* with accompanying foreword by Pia Gilbert, New York: American Music Center, 250 W. 57.

Horst, Louis. *Three South American Dances.* New York: Orchesis Publications, (200 West 57th St.)

Horst, Louis. *Comin' Round The Mountain.* New York: Orchesis Publications, (200 West 57th St.)

Horst, Louis. *Music For Dance Technique.* New York: Louis Horst, 55 West 11th St.

Jahn, Daniel. *Seven Pre-Classic Dances.* New York: Motif Publications, 200 West 57th St.

Jahn, Daniel. *Eleven Choreographic Etudes.* New York: Motif Publications, 200 West 57th St.

Lloyd, Norman. *Accompaniments For Modern Dance and Supplements.* New York: Norman Lloyd, 41 Grove St.

Miller, Freda. *Romantic and Contemporary Dances.* New York: Freda Miller, 237 East 81st Street.

Walberg, Betty Horner. *Accompaniment Studies.* New York: Betty Horner Walberg, 213 East 51st Street.

RECORDINGS

It is important to keep abreast of the recording industry. At present, extensive recording is being done in stereophonic sound. This means that many of the numbers now currently listed will be changed as the music is re-recorded. It also means that some prudent shopping at a time of change such as this may result in considerable savings.

The following list of recordings was chosen in order to meet varying needs. In some cases a department now offers a broad range of dance classes, such as an extensive course in dance history; beginning, intermediate, and advanced composition; various sections of technique on different levels; and courses in philosophy and in methods of teaching dance. In this event, a wide range of recordings is necessary, and the following list in its entirety, therefore, is suggested as a minimum catalogue of basic records that should be available.

On the other hand, most teachers, dancers, and departments are considerably more limited. For the many who are now in the process of building a recording library and yet must consider the limitations of a budget, a priority system for rating the following list of records has been devised. This rating is not in terms of quality, for all of the records listed are of high standard, but rather in terms of immediate need and practicability.

Four categories are indicated, therefore, in the following list of recordings:

***—essential, basic

** —highly recommended

* —desirable

no marking—should be purchased eventually.

Record labels have been abbreviated as follows:

All.	Allegro
Ang.	Angel
Aud.	Audio-Drama
Cam.	Camden
Cap.	Capital
Classic	Classic
Col.	Columbia
Con.	Concord
CPS-CRI.	Composers Recordings (Harte)
CPT.	Counterpoint
Dec.	Decca
Edu.	Educo
E.M.S.	Educational Music Series
Epic	Epic
H.	Concert Hall
Heritage	Heritage
Lon.	London

Lyr.	Lyric
Mer.	Mercury
MGM.	MGM Records
Mus.Lib.	Modern Music Library
Per.	Period
Rem.	Remington
Ren.	Renaissance Records
SPA.	SPA Records
STV.	Stradivari
Uni.	Unicorn
Urania	Urania
Van.	Vanguard
Vic.	RCA Victor
Vox	Vox
Walden	Walden
WSH.	Washington
West.	Westminster
Zodiac	Zodiac

Recordings Specially Selected for Modern Dance

ANTHEIL GEORGE (1900-
Ballet Mecanique (1925)
Surinach, N.Y. Percussion Group + Brant............
....Col. ML-4956
Sonato No. 2 for Violin & Piano (1923)
Israel Baker, Yaltah Menuhin.............Mus-Lib. 7006

BACH, JOHANN SEBASTIAN (1685-1750)
Casals, Prades Festival Orch. 3-Col. ML-4345/7
....3-Col. ML-4345/7
Casals, Prades Festival Orch. +Brandenburg 1, 2........
....Col. ML-4345
**English Suites (6) for Harpischord
Valenti.......................2-West 18384/5
**French Suites (6) for Harpischord
Valenti.......................2-West 18157/8
***Inventions, 2 Part
Landowska (harpischord) +Con. 1.......Vic. LM-1974
Italian Concerto for Harpischord
Serkin (piano) +Cello Son 3; Chrom...Col. ML 4350
Suite No. 2 in b for Flute and Strings
Barwahser, Van Beinum, Concertgebouw Orchestra
Suites 1,3,4.......................2 Epic SC-6024

BARBER, SAMUEL (1910-
Adagio for Strings: Essay for Orchestra No. 11 Overture:
School for Scandal (1933) Op. 5
Hanson, Eastman-Rochester Sym+Sym 1....Mer. 50148
Sonata for Cello and Piano Op. 6 (1932)
Piatigorsky, Berkowitz+Hindemith-Sonata for Cello &
Piano.......................Vic. LM-2013

BARTOK, BELA (1881-1945)
**Bela Bartok Plays Bartok
Bartok (piano).......................Rem. 94
**Dance Suite (1923)
Pfluger, Leipzig Phil + Prokofiev Prodigal....Urania 7173
***For Children Vol 1 & 2 (1908)
Anda (& Sonatina).......................2-Ang. 35126, 35246
**Mikrokosmos (excerpts)
Bartok.......................Col. ML-4419
**Music for Strings, Percussion, Celesta (1935)
Van Beinum, Concertgebouw Orch + Stravinsky
Song of the Nightingale.......................Epic LC-3274
Out of Doors Suite (1926)
Hambro + Improvisations.......................VRS 902

Quartets Nos. 5 (1934) & 6 (1939)
Juillard Quarter................Col. ML-4280
*Sonata for 2 Pianos and Percussion (1937)
Brendel, Zeika, Reinhardt, Pro Musica Orch +
Music............,..................Vox 9600

BEETHOVEN, LUDVIG VAN (1770-1827)
*Bagatelles
Foldes (& Andante, Fur Elise, Ecossaises in E) +
Var. Grove 191................Dec. 9964
Piano Music
Balsam.......................WSH. 401
Variations on a Theme by Diabelli Op. 120
Serkin.......................Col. ML-5246
Viennese Dances
Litschauer, Vienna St. Op. Orch + Contra Dances
.......................Van. 429

BERG, ALBAN (1885-1935)
***Quartet. Op. 3 (1910)
Juillard Quartet + Schonberg: Quartet 4 Webern
................Col. ML-4737

BERNSTEIN, LEONARD (1918-
Facsimile (1946)
Bernstein RCA Victor Sym + Jeremiah (& On the
Town).......................Cam. 196
Fancy Free (1944)
Bernstein, Columbia Sym + Copland-Salon: Milhaud:
Creation.......................Col. CL-920

BLOCH, ERNEST (1880-
Con. Grosso for String Orch & Piano (1924-5)
Franklin, Steinberg Pittsburgh Sym + W Schumann-
Symphony for Strings................Cap. P-8212

BOULEZ, PIERRE (1925-
Le Martean Sans Maitre.......Col. ML-5275

BOWLES, PAUL (1910-
*Music for A Farce: Scenes d'Anabase (1932)
Glazer, Muller, Bailey; Hess, Marx Masselos (f) +
Dello Joio.......................Col. ML 4845

BRAHMS, JOHANNES (1833-1897)
Liebeslieder Waltzes
Boulanger, Ens. (G) (Op. 65 & Songs)......Dec. 9650
Piano Music
Rubinstein (from Op. 76, 79, 117, 118, 119)........
.......................Vic. LM-1787
Sonata No. 3 in f for Piano Op. 5
Badura-Skoda.......................West 18447

BRANT, HENRY (1913-
Concerto for Saxophone & Orchestra (1941)
Rascher, Johnson, Cincinnati Sym + Rudhyar:
Glansville-Hicks.......................Rem. 188

BRITTEN, BENJAMIN (1913-
Peter Grimes: 4 Sea Interludes & Passacaglia Op. 33A
(1944)
Van Beinum Concertgebouw Orch + Young Person's
Guide.......................Lon. LL-917

BYRD, WILLIAM (1543-1623)
Motets
Howard, Renaissance Singers (L).........West. 18402

CARTER, ELLIOTT (1908-
The Minotaur (ballet suite)
Hanson, Eastman-Rochester Sym + McPhee.........
.......................Mer. 50103

CASTELNUOVO-TEDESCO, MARIO (1895-
Quintet for Guitar & String Quartet Op. 143
Segovia, Quintetto Chigiano Strings (See Col.
Guitar).......................Dec. 9832

CHOPIN, FREDERIC (1810-1849)
*Etudes, Op. 19 and Op. 25
Novaes (Op. 10 & Scherzo 1).......Vox 9070
*Mazurkas
Horowitz + Schumann: Kinderscenen....Vic. LVT-1032
**Preludes (24), Op. 28
Rubenstein.......................Vic. LM-1163
Waltzes
Rubenstein.......................Vic. LM-1892

COPLAND, AARON (1900-
*Billy the Kid (ballet suite, 1938)
Ormandy, Phila Orch + Appalachian....Col. ML-5157
*Music for the Theatre (1925)
Solomon, MGM Orch + Weill.......MGM 3095
*Rodeo (1942)
Dorati, Mpls, Sym + Danzon: Salon........Mer. 50172
*Salon Mexico El (1936)
Bernstein, Columbia Sym + Milhaud: Creation
Bernstein.......................Col. CL-920
*Variations for Piano (1930) Passecaglia (1922)
Aitken + Son.......................Walden 101

CORELLI, ARCANGELO (1653-1713)
La Follia
Grumlaux, Castagnone + Tartini-Son. "Devil's Trill"
Veracini: Vitali.......................Epic LC-3414

COUPERIN, FRANCOIS (1668-1733)
Ballet Suite in G
Desarzens, Lausanne Ch Orch + Rameau: Platee
.......................Con. H-1523
*Harpischord Music
Marlowe.......................Rem. 202

COWELL, HENRY (1897-
**Piano Music: Prelude for Violin & Harpischord
Cowell: Brink, Pinkham + Hovhaness: Pinkham
.......................CPS-CRI 109

CRESTON, PAUL (1906-
*Invocation & Dance
Whitney, Louisville Orch + Ibert: Louisville Concerto;
Cowell: Sym 11.......................Col. ML-5039

DAHL, INGOLF (1912-
*Allegro and Arioso
New Art Wind Quintet + Carter; Cowell: Boeb;
Perischetti; Piston: Riegger.......2-Classic 2003
*Music for Brass Instruments
Voisin, Ens. + Hindemith: Morgenmusik; Berezowski:
Brass Suite
Sanders: Qn.......................Uni. 1031

DEBUSSY, CLAUDE (1862-1918)
*Children's Corner Suite
Casadesus (see Debussy Piano).......Col. ML-4978
Piano Music
Gieseking.......................Ang. 35026
*Pour le Piano
Gieseking + Estampes: Images.......Ang. 35065
Sonata No. 3 in g for Violin and Piano
Francescatti Casadesus + Franck: Sonata.......
.......................Col. ML-4178

DELLO JOIO, NORMAN (1913-
**Sonata No. 3 for Piano
Del Purves + Griffes.......Mus-Lib. 7021

DOHNANYI, ERNST VON (1877-
Rhapsodies (4) for Piano Op. 11
Dohnanyi + Schumann: Kinderscenen.......Rem. 43

DVORAK, ANTONIN (1841-1904)
Slavonic Dances
Talich, Cxech Phil (Op. 46).......Urania 7076

EGK, WERNER (1901-
French Suite After Rameau
Fricsay, RIAS Sym + Hartmann..................Dec. 9861

FALLA, MANUEL DE (1876-1946)
Three Cornered Hat: Dances (Cont'd)
Mitropoulos, NY Phil + Nights in the Gardens of Spain
Vida Breve.......................................Col. ML-5172
Vida Breve; Interlude & Dance
Dorati, Mpls Sym + Albeniz-Iberia..........Mer. 50146

FAURE, GABRIEL (1845-1924)
Trio in d, Op. 120
Beaux-Arts Trio + Ravel; Trio.................MGM 3455

FINE, IRVING (1914-
*Partita for Woodwind Quintet
New Art Quintet + Milhaud; Sketches; Berezowsky
Suite...Classic 1003

FRANCAIX, JEAN (1912-
Concertino for Piano & Orchestra (1932)
Weber, Fricsay, Berlin Radio Sym + Honegger
Concertino; R. Strauss; Burleske.................Dec. 9900

FRESCOBALDI, DIROLAMO (1583-1643)
***Harpischord Music
Marlow + D. Scarlatti; Sonatas................Cap. P-8336

GERSHWIN, GEORGE (1898-1937)
Music of George Gershwin
Gershwin Plays.....................10" Heritage 0073
***Preludes for Piano
Gould + Rhapsody; Concerto; American in Paris
Porgy and Bess...............................Vic. LM-6033

GLUCK, CHRISTOPH WILLIBALD (1714-1787)
Ballet Suite (arr. Motti)
Irving London Sym + Gretry..............Lon. LL-1234

GRIEG, EDVARD (1843-1907)
Lyric Pieces
Gieseking (Albums 1,2)...................2-Ang. 35450/1

GRIFFES, CHARLES TOMLINSON (1884-1920)
**Three Short Pieces
Ranck (piano) + Poulenc; Soirees; Tcherepnin;
Werle...Zodiac 1002

HAIEFF, ALEXEI (1914-
*Juke Box Pieces; 5 Piano Pieces
Leo Smit + Concerto..........................MGM 3243
Quartet No. 1
Juilliard Qr + Barber; Hermit...............Col. ML-4988

HANDEL, GEORGE FREDERICK (1685-1759)
Harmonious Blacksmith
Landowska (see Col. Harpischord).......Vic. LM-1217
Sonatas for Flute, Oboe & Continuo
Kaplan, Schaefer, Holmes Bodky..............All. 59

HARRIS, ROY (1898-
Sonata for Violin & Piano (1942)
Gingold J, Harris + Palmer...............Col. ML-4842

HARRISON, LOU (1917-
*Suite for Violin, Piano & Small Orchestra
A. & M. Ajemian, Stokowski, Sym Orch + Cowell;
Persian..................................CPS-CRI 114

HAYDN, FRANZ JOSEF (1732-1809)
Concerto in G for Cembalo and Orchestra
E. & A. Heiller, Vienna Coll. Mus. Orch + Organ
Con..............................Hayden Society 9023
Sonatas for Piano
Kraus (Nos. 5, 9)..............................Edu. 3005

HINDEMITH, PAUL (1895-
*Five Pieces for String Orch. Op. 44, No. 4 (1927)
Goldberg, Netherlands Ch. Orch + Theme;
Trauermusik...............................Epic LC-3356
*Kleine Kammermusik, Op. 24, No. 2 (1922)
Fine Arts Wind Ens. + Poulenc: Sextet ...Cap. P-8258
*Sonata for Clarinet & Piano (1939)
Kell, Rosen + Debussy; Premiere; Stravinsky,
Three Pieces...............................Dec. 9570
*Sonata No. 3 for Piano (1936)
Badura-Skoda + Sonata 1...................West. 18200

HOVHANESS, ALAN (1911-
*Duet for Violin & Harpischord
Brink, Pinkham + Cowell; Pinkham........CPS-CRI 109
*Prelude & Quadruple Fugue
Hanson, Eastman-Rochester Sym. + Lo Presti;
Sessions.......................................Mer. 50106

IBERT, JACQUES (1890-
Divertissement
Fantasque.................................Vic. LM 2084
Trois Pieces Breves
Chicago Sym. Woodwind Qn. Hindemith: Kleine;
Milhaud; Cheminee............................Aud. 15

IVES, CHARLES (1874-1954)
**The Unanswered Question (1908)
Foss, Zimbler Sinfon + Bartok: Divert; Milhaud; Sym.;
Skalkottas......................................Uni. 1037

JOSTEN, WERNER (1885-
*Sonatina for Violin & Piano
Elman, Seiger + Achron; Block; Nigun; Korngold
....Lon. LL-1467

KABALEVSKY, SMITRI (1904-
Preludes (24)
Reisenberg...................................West. 18095

KOHS, ELLIS (1916-
Chamber Concerto for Viola & String Nonet
Molnar, San Fran. Sym. Members.......Mus. Lib. 7004

KRENEK, ERNST (1900-
Four Bagatelles (Sonata Op. 70)
Krenek, Ajemian + Sonata 4...........Mus. Lib. 7014
**Sonata No. 3 (1943) Piano Pieces
Krenek..SPA 4

LANNER, JOSEF (1801-1843)
Waltzes
Paulik, Vienna St. Op. Or. + Strauss Sr........Van. 458

LIEBERMANN, ROLF (1910-
Concerto for Jazz Band & Orchestra
Reiner, Sauter-Finegan Orch. Chicago Sym. + R.
Strauss: Don Juan.........................Vic. LM-1888

LOPATNIKOFF, NIKOLAI (1903-
Variations & Epilogue for Cello & Piano
N. J. Graudan + Glanville-Hicks..........Col. ML-4990

McBRIDE, ROBERT (1911-
Aria & Toccata in Swing (1946-
Kaufman + Carpenter, Copland Still Con.......H-1640

MENDELSSOHN, FELIX (1809-1847)
Songs Without Words
Gieseking...................................Ang. 35428

MENNIN, PETER (1923)
Quartet No. 2
Juilliard Quartet + Imbrie.................Col. ML-4844

MILHAUD, DARIUS (1892-
Concerto for Percussion & Small Orch (1930)............
....Col. ML-5129
Creation du Monde
Bernstein, Columbia Sym + Copland Salon, Mexico;
Bernstein; Fancy Free...................Col. CL-920
**Saudades Do Brasil (1920-21)
Milhaud, Concert Arts Orch + Suite.......Cap. P-8358
Sketches (2) for Woodwind Quintet
New Art Quintet + Berezowski.............Classic 1003

MOMPOU, FEDERICO (1893-
**Piano Pieces
Mompou...Ang. 35147

MOZART, WOLFGANG AMADEUS (1756-1791)
German Dances
Gieseking (K, 509) (see Mozart; Piano)....Ang. 35078
Petits Riens, Les (ballet music) App. 10
Braithwaite, Royal Op. Orch + D. Scarlatti
Good Humored Ladies.............................MGM 3034
Piano Music (complete)
Gieseking 11-Ang. 3512-C (35068)/78)...........$75.00

NORTH, ALEX (1910-
**Holiday Set
Adler, Vienna Orch + Antheil; Cowell; Jacobi;
Siegmeister..SPA 47

OFFENBACH, JACQUES (1819-1880)
Belle Helene, La (excerpts)
Leibowitz, Paris Phil (F) + Orpheus..........Ren. X-51
Bluebeard (ballet-arr. Dorati)
Levine, Ballet Theatre Orch + Helen.......Cap. P-8277
Gaite Parisienne
Dorati, Mpls Sym + J. Strauss; Graduation Mer. 50152

ORFF, CARL (1895-
Carmina Burana (scenic cantata) (1935-36)
Mahler, Hartford Sym & Cho (G.L.)...........Van. 1007

PERSICHETTI, VINCENT (1915-
*Divertimento for Band
Fennel, Eastman Sym Wind Ens. + Gould; Schuman;
Piston; Barber; Bennett.......................Mer. 50079

POULENC, FRANCIS (1899-
*Sonata for Two Pianos (1953)
Gold & Fixdale + Bowles; Picnic...........Col. ML-5068
Trio for Trumpet, Trombone, Horn (1922)
Glantz, Pulis, Berv + Saint Saens.............STV. 605

PROKOFIEV, SERG (1891-1953)
Buffoon, Suite No. 1 Op. 21 (1921)
Golschmann, St. Louis Sym + Falla; Three Cornered
Hat..Cap. P-8257
Cinderella (excerpts) (1941-44)
Pressler + Piano Sonata 9........... ....MGM 3192
Classical Symphony in D, Op. 25 (1916-17)
Steinberg, Pittsburgh Sym + Tchaikovsky-Serenade
....Cap. P-8290
***Music for Children, Op. 65 (1935)
Pressler + Bloch; Milhaud; Starer; Shostakovitch
....MGM 3010
**Piano Music
Prokofiev (5-58) + Con. 3....................Ang. 34
*Sonata No. 7 for Piano, Op. 83 (1940)
Nadas + Bartok; Son; Bloch Son Stravinsky Son
....Per. 736

PURCELL, HENRY (c. 1659-1695)
Fantasias (4 part) Chaconne in g
Litschauer, Vienna Ch. Or.......................Van. 420
Sonata in D for Trumpet & Strings; Trumpet

*Voluntary in D; Tune & Air for Trumpet
Voisin, Dickson, Unicorn Concert Orch + Voluntaries;
Haydn; Trumpet Con; Vivaldi: 2 Trumpet Con
....Uni. 1054

RAMEAU, JEAN PHILIPPE (1683-1764)
Harpsichord Works (complete)
Veyron-Lacroix.................3-West. 3303 (18124/6)

RAVEL, MAURICE (1875-1937)
*Piano Music
Casadesus.......................................Col. ML-5213
Quartet in F (1920)
Budapest Quartet + Debussy; Qr........Col. ML-5245
*Sonatine for Piano (1903-05)
Gieseking (see Ravel: Piano)...............3-Ang. 3541-5S
Tombeau de Couperin, le (1914-17)
Gieseking (see Ravel: Piano).................3-Ang. 3541
*Trio in a (piano) (1915)
Rubinstein, Heifetz, Piatigorsky + Mendelssohn:
Trio...Vic. LM-1119
La Valse (1920)
Ormandy...Col. ML-4983

RIEGGER, WALLINGFORD (1885-
**New Dance (1934)
Hanson, Eastman-Rochester Sym + Cowell; Cym. 4
Hovhaness; Con. 1................................Mer. 50078
Quintet Op. 51
New Art Wind Quintet + Carter; Cowell; Goeb;
Dahl; Persichetti; Piston 2-Classic 2003
Sonatina for Violin & Piano
A. & M. Ajemian + Krenck: Sessions ......MGM 3218

RIETI, VITTORIO (1898-
*Dance Variations for String Orchestra
Surinach, MGM String Orch + Rozsa.......MGM 3565
Sonata all' Antica
Marlowe + Hovhaness; Lessard; Thomson..............
....Dec. New Ed. 3

ROUSSEL, ALBERT (1869-1937)
Trio for Flute, Viola, Cello, Op. 40
Baker, L. & H. Fuchs + Debussy; Son.......Dec. 9777

SATIE, ERIK (1866-1925)
Piano Music
Ciccolini...Ang. 35442
Three Pieces in the Shape of a Pear (1903)
Robert & Gaby Casadesus + Saint-Saens Piano Con.
4..Col. ML-4246

SCARLATTI, DOMENICO (1685-1757)
***Sonatas for Harpsichord
Kirkpatrick...4-Col. SL-221

SCHOENBERG, ARNOLD (1874-1951)
Chamber Symphony No. 2. Op. 38
Haffner, Vienna Sym + Survivor............Col. ML-4664
**Piano Music
Steuermann (complete) (12-57)...........Col. ML-5216
Quartet No. 4 Op. 37 (1936)
Juillard Quartet + Berg; Webern............Col. ML-4737
**Suite. Op. 29 (1934)
Schuller Septet......................................Per. 705

SCHUBERT, FRANZ (1797-1828)
German Dances
Litschauer, Vienna St. Op. Orch + Mozart Serenade;
K 525...Van. 435
Impromptus
Lipatti (Op. 90) (see Col. Piano)...........2-Ang. 3556B
Laendler, Op. 171
Flesher + Sonata in B ♭......................Col. ML-5061
Quintet in A, Op. 114 "Trout"
Festival Quartet, Sankey.......................Vic. LM-2147

SCHULLER, GUNTHER (1925-
**Symphony for Brass & Percussion, Op. 16 (1950)
Mitropoulos, Brass Ens. (see Jass, Brass Ens)
....Col. CL-941

SCHUMAN, WILLIAM (1910-
Undertow, Choreographic Episodes (1945)
Levine Ballet Th. Or. + Copland; Billy....Cap. P-8238

SCHUMANN, ROBERT (1810-1856)
Carnaval, Op. 9
Casadesus + Fantasia....................Col. ML-5146
Davidsbundler Dances, Op. 6
Firkusny + Sym Etudes...................Cap. P-8337
Horowitz + Chopin, Mazurkas.............Vic. LVT-1032

SHOSTAKOVITCH, DMITRI (1906-
Ballet Russe
Kurtz Columbia Sym + Tchaikovsky; Serenade
Melancolique..................Col. ML-4671
Golden Age. Op. 22 (Ballet Suite, 1929-30)
Mitchell, Nat'l Sym + Sym 1...............West. 18293
***Preludes (24) Op. 34 (1932-33)
Menahem Pressler........................MGM 3070
Quintet (piano) Op. 57 (1940)
Aller, Hollywood Quartet.................Cap. P-81 71

SMETANA, FRIEDRICH (1824-1884)
Czech Polkas & Dances
Firkusny.................................Cap. P-8372
Trio in g (Piano) Op. 15
Oistrakh, Knushevitsky, Oborin + Dvorak; Trio in e
..................................West. 18175

STRAUSS, JOHANN (1825-1899)
*Beau Danube (Ballet)
Rosenthal, Paris Opera Orch.............Cap. P-18006
*Graduation Ball
Fiedler, Boston Pops + Chopin; Sylphides..............
.............................Vic. LM-1919
*Polkas
Paulik, Vienna St. Op. Orch..............Van. 438
*Waltzes
Reiner, Pittsburgh Sym Orch + Brahms-Hungarian
Dances...............................Col. ML-4116

STRAUSS, RICHARD (1864-1949)
Burleske In D (1885)
Serkin, Ormandy, Phila Orch + Schumann Con
.................................Col. ML-5168
*Dance Suite after Couperin
Kloss, Frankenland St., Sym.............Lyr. 58
Death and Transfiguration, Op. 24 (1889)
Knappertsbusch, Orch Paris Consv. + Don Juan
................................Lon. LL-1478

STRAVINSKY, IGOR (1822-
**Agon (Ballet)
Stravinsky, Los Angeles Fest. Sym + Canticum Sacrum
.................................Col. ML-5215
**Le Baiser de la Fée (1928)
Stravinsky, Cleveland Orch.............Col. ML-5102
**Danses Concertantes (1942)
Stravinsky, RCA Vic. Ch. Orch + Baiser de la Fee
...............................Vic. LVT-1029
**Duo Concertant for Violin & Piano (1932)
Fuchs Smit + Copland; Vn. Sonata.........Dec. 8503
**Firebird Suite
Goehr, Netherlands Phil. + Falla; Amor Con. RG-128
**L'Histoire du Soldat, Suite
Stravinsky, Ens. + Octet; Sym for Winds.............
.................................Col. ML-4964
**Jeu de Cartes (1936)
Hollreiser, Bamberg Sym + Vn. Con; Duo....Vox 9410

**Petrouchka (1911)
Kurtz, Phil. Orch....................Ang. 35552
**Pulcinella Suite (1920)
Ansermet, Orch, Suisse Romande + Song of the
Nightingale.......................Lon. LL-1494
**Sacre du Printemps, Le (1913)
Ormandy, Phila Orch + Petrouchka......Col. ML-5030
**Sonata for Piano (1924)
S. Stravinsky (& Serenade) + Ravel..........All. 3091

TCHAIKOVSKY, PETER ILICH (1840-1893)
Nutcracker Suite, Op. 71 A
Dorati, Mpls. Sym + Britten; Young......Mer. 50055
Sleeping Beauty Ballet (excerpts)
Monteux, London Sym...................Vic. LM-2177
Swan Lake Ballet (excerpts)
Von Karajan, Phil. Orch + Sleeping.......Ang. 35006

TCHEREPNIN, ALEXANDER (1899-
**Bagatelles (10)
Ranck (piano) + Griffes: 3 short pieces: Poulenc
Soirees; Werle....................Zodiac 1002

THOMSON, VIRGIL (1896-
Filling Station (1938)
Barzin, N.Y.C. Ballet Orch + Kay.............Vox 9050
Louisiana Story: Acadian Songs & Dances
Scherman, Little Orch, Soc. + Copland......Dec. 9616

TOCH, ERNST (1887-
Renzi, Surinach, MGM Ch. Orch (E) + M. Richter
....MGM 3546
***Ten Studies for Beginners. Op. 59
Richter + Hindemith: Twelve Pieces Surinach; Satie;
Hovhaness.........................MGM 3181

VAUGHAN WILLIAMS, RALPH (1872-
English Folk Song Suite
Boult, Phil. Prom. Orch + Greensleeves: Fantasia
Norfolk Rhapsody..................West. 18248
Toccata Marziale
Fennell, Eastman Wind Ens. + English Folk Song
Suite; Hoist.......................Mer. 50088

VILLA-LOBOS, HEITOR (1887-
Bachianas Brasileiras No. 5 for Soprano & Celli (1938)
De Los Angeles, Benedetti, Villa-Lobos, Orch
Nat'l Radio, Fr. + Bachianas 2,6,9.........Ang. 35547
**Piano Music
Jacques Abram....................,.........EMS 10

VIVALDI, ANTONIO (c. 1675-1741)
Concerti for Two Violins and Orchestra (Cont'd)
D. & I. Oistrakh, Konwitschny, Leipzig Gewandhaus
Orch (in a Op. 3/8) + Bach: 2 Vn Con., Trio
Son in C: Tartini: Trio Son ....Dec. 9950

WEBERN, ANTON (1883-1945)
**Five Movements for String Quartet, Op. 5 (1909)
Juilliard Quartet + Schonberg: Quartet 4; Berg
.................................Col. ML-4737
Complete Works
Robert Craft.......................Col. K4L-232

WEILL, KURT (1900-1950)
Seven Deadly Sins (Ballet in Song)
Lenya, Bruckner-Ruggeberg, Male Quartet & Orch (G)
.................................Col. KL-5175

WOLPE, STEFAN (1902-
*Quartet for Percussion
Baron, Ch. Group + Sonata.............Es. 530

Recordings Specifically Designed for Modern Dance

Gilbert, Pia. *Music for Dance*, with accompanying
booklet of suggestions for using the record by Aileene

Lockhart. (LP) Los Angeles: Children's Music Center, 5373 W. Pico Blvd. (The major portion of the musical score which is recorded on this record is published in the book, *Music for the Modern Dance*).

Johnson, Hazel. *Music for Rhythms.* New York: Hazel Johnson, 123 W. 13th Street.

Merrill, Kathleen. *Studies and Sketches for Modern Dance.* Miami: Kathleen Merrill, 6484 S. W. 25th Street.

Miller, Freda D. *Accompaniment for Dance Technique.* New York: Freda D. Miller, 237 East 81st Street.

Miller, Freda D. *A Second Album of Dance.* New York: Freda D. Miller, 237 East 81st Street.

Miller, Freda D. *Third Album for Dance.* New York: Freda D. Miller, 237 East 81st Street.

Miller, Freda D. *Music for Rhythms and Dance.* New York: Freda D. Miller, 237 East 81st Street.

Moore, Fredericka. *Rhythm Is Fun.* Los Angeles: Bowmar Records, 4921 Santa Monica Blvd.

Throckmorton, Dillon W. and Maxin A. Roberts. *Music for Orchesis.* Manhattan Beach, California: Throckmorton and Roberts, 3524 Palm Ave.

Van Deman, Mary O. *Four Studies for Dance Composition.* San Carlos, California: Fredericka Moore, 2633 Graceland Ave.

SELECTED REFERENCES

Andrews, Gladys. *Creative Rhythmic Movement for Children.* New York: Prentice-Hall Inc., 1954. Chapter 9, "Percussion and Movement."

Arvey, Verna. *Choreographic Music.* New York: E. P. Dutton and Co., 1941.

Beiswanger, George. "Music at the Bennington Festival." *Dance Observer,* Vol. V (August-September 1938), pp. 102-104.

Bernstein, Leonard. "Music and the Dance." *Dance,* (June 1946), pp. 28, 42.

Boas, Franziska. "Notes on Percussion Accompaniment for the Dance." *Dance Observer, Vol.* V (May 1938), pp. 71-72.

Boas, Franziska. "Percussion Music and Its Relation to the Modern Dance." *Dance Observer,* Vol. VII (January 1940), pp. 6-7.

Cage, John and William Russell. "Percussion Music and Its Relation to Modern Dance." *Dance Observer,* Vol. VI (October 1939), pp. 296, 274.

Coleman, Satis. *The Drum Book.* New York: John Day Co., 1931.

Copland, Aaron. *What to Listen For In Music.* New York: McGraw-Hill Book Co., 1939.

Cowell, Henry. "How Relate Music and Dance." *Dance Observer,* Vol. I (June-July 1934), p. 52.

Cowell, Henry. "New Sounds in Music for the Dance." *Dance Observer,* Vol. VIII (May 1941), pp. 64, 70.

Cowell, Henry. "Relating Music and Concert Dance." *Dance Observer,* Vol. IV (January 1937), pp. 1, 7-8

Cowell, Henry. "Music at Bennington." *Dance Observer,* Vol. VIII (August-September 1941), pp. 96-97.

Cowell, Henry and John Cage. "Percussion Music and Its Relation to the Modern Dance." *Dance Observer,* Vol. VI (November 1939), pp. 296-297.

Dewsnup, Maurine. "Dancers Face the Music." *Journal of Health, Physical Education and Recreation* (February 1956), pp. 44-45, 60.

Dietrich, Sally Tobin. "Accompaniment for Tap Dance." *Educational Dance,* Vol. II (March 1940), pp. 4-5.

Dlugoszewski, Lucia. "Notes on New Music for the Dance." *Dance Observer,* Vol. XXIV (November 1957), pp. 133-135.

Dorn, Gerhardt. "Music for Dance Production." *Educational Dance,* Vol. III (January 1941), pp. 10-11.

Dorn, Gerhardt. "Music Improvisation for the Dance." *Educational Dance,* Vol. II (August-September 1939), pp. 7-8.

Dorn, Gerhardt. "Nature and Use of Primitive Music." *Educational Dance,* Vol. IV (October 1941), pp. 8-9.

Dorn, Gerhardt. "Music for Social Dance." *Educational Dance,* Vol. IV (December 1941), p. 10.

Dougherty, John. "Music for Dance." *Dance Magazine,* Vol. XXXII (November 1958), pp. 14-15, 80-82.

Duggan, Anne S. "Modern Dance and Music: Related Arts." *The Southwestern Musician,* (January-February 1943), p. 5.

Engel, Lehman. "Choric Sounds for the Dance." *Dance Observer,* Vol. I (April 1934), p. 29.

Engel, Lehman. "Music for the Dance." *Dance Observer,* Vol. I (February 1934), pp. 4-8.

Erlanger, Margaret (coordinator). *Materials for Teaching Dance.* Vol. I. Washington, D.C.: National Section on Dance, American Association for Health, Physical Education and Recreation, 1953.

Flade, Tina. "Use of Percussion Instruments in Dance Accompaniment." *Journal of Health and Physical Education,* (February 1935), p. 19.

Foehrenbach, Lenore M. "Musical Accompaniment for High School Modern Dance." *Journal of Health, Physical Education and Recreation,* (June 1950), pp. 327-328, 370-372.

Galea, Manuel. "Music and the Ballet." *Educational Dance,* Vol. IV (January 1942), pp. 5-7.

Gilbert, Pia. "Fitting Music to Dance." *Journal of Health, Physical Education and Recreation,* (March 1953), pp. 11-12.

Graham, Harriet. "A Study of the Use of Percussion Instruments as Accompaniment in the Dance." *Research Quarterly* of the American Association for Health, Physical Education and Recreation, Vol. V (March 1934), pp. 12-30.

Green, Ray. "Music and Dance Perspective." *Dance Observer,* Vol. V (October 1938), p. 118.

Harrison, Lou. "Percussion Music and Its Relation to the Modern Dance." *Dance Observer,* Vol. VII (March 1940), p. 32.

Hastings, Baird. "Music and Theatrical Dance." *Educational Dance,* Vol. IV (August-September 1941), pp. 3-4.

Hawkins, Alma. *"Current Personnel and Practices Relative to the Dance Accompanist-Composer in Selected Colleges and Universities."* Unpublished study, University of California at Los Angeles, 1959.

Hayes, Elizabeth R. *Dance Composition and Production.* New York: A. S. Barnes and Co., 1955. Chapter 9, "Music and Percussion Accompaniment for Dance."

H'Doubler, Margaret H. *Dance—A Creative Art Experience.* New York: F. S. Crofts and Co., 1940. Chapter 8. "Dance and Music."

Hellebrandt, Beatrice. "Musical Percussion—Its Place in Modern Dance Education." *Journal of Health and Physical Education,* Vol. VIII (May 1937), pp. 290-293.

Hellebrandt, Beatrice. "Rhythmics in Music and Dance." *Research Quarterly* of the American Association for Health, Physical Education and Recreation, Vol. XI (March 1940), pp. 34-39.

Heynssen, Adda. *Modern Dance Accompaniment: Relationship of Music and Dance.* London: J. Curwen and Sons; New York: G. Schirmer, Inc.

Hill, Martha. "An Analysis of Accompaniment for the Dance." Chapter 7 in *Dancing in the Elementary Schools* by the Committees on Dancing of the American Physical Education Association. New York: A. S. Barnes and Co., 1933, pp. 87-106.

Horst, Louis. "Modern Forms: Introduction." *Dance Observer.* Vol. VI (November 1939), p. 285.

Horst, Louis. "Modern Forms. Understanding by Contrast: Rhythm." *Dance Observer,* Vol. VI (December 1939), pp. 298-299.

Horst, Louis. "Modern Forms. Understanding by Contrast: Melodic Linear Design." *Dance Observer,* Vol. VIII (February 1941), p. 23.

Horst, Louis. "Music and Dance." *Dance Observer,* Vol. II (May 1935), p. 1.

Horst, Louis. *Pre-Classic Dance Forms.* New York: Kamin Dance Publishers, 1954.

Horst, Louis. "Modern Forms. Understanding by Contrast: Harmonic Texture." *Dance Observer,* Vol. X (August-September 1943), p. 79.

House, Gladys R. "The Folk Dance Accompanist." *Journal of Health, Physical Education and Recreation,* (May 1953), pp. 27-28.

Howard, John T. *Our Contemporary Composers.* New York: Thomas Y. Crowell Co., 1941.

Howard, John T. and James Lyons. *Modern Music.* New York: Mentor Books, 1957.

Hungerford, Mary Jane. "Basic Rhythms." *Educational Dance,* Vol. II (November 1939), pp. 3-5; (January 1940), pp. 5-7.

Joel, Lydia. "The Waltz That Wouldn't Stay Banned." *Dance,* Vol. XXIV (November 1950), pp. 30-31.

Johnston, Ben. "Music and Dance With the Spoken Word." *Dance Observer,* Vol. XIX (August-September 1952), pp. 100-101.

Kinnaird, Muriel Louella. *A Survey of Special Courses in Accompaniment for Movement, and/or Units of Study in Accompaniment within Modern Dance Classes, and Accompaniment in General for Modern Dance Classes in Selected Colleges and Universities in the United States.* Unpublished M.A. thesis, Texas State College for Women, 1956.

Lambert, Constant. *Music Ho!* Baltimore: Penquin Books Ltd.

Leichtentritt, Hugo. *Musical Form.* Cambridge: Harvard University Press, 1956.

Lippincott, Gertrude (editor). *Dance Production.* Washington, D.C.: National Section on Dance of the American Association for Health, Physical Education and Recreation. Chapter 5 "Selection of Music," pp. 39-49.

Lloyd, Norman. "Music in the Gymnasium I, II." *Journal of Health, Physical Education and Recreation,* Vol. XI. (January 1940), pp. 15, 62; (March 1940), pp. 142-143, 193-194.

Lloyd, Ruth and Norman Lloyd. "Music for the Dance." *Dance Observer,* Vol. V (June-July 1938), pp. 84-85.

Lloyd, Norman. "American Composers Write for the Dance." *Dance Observer,* Vol. XVIII (November 1951), pp. 132-134.

Lloyd, Ruth and Norman Lloyd. "Accompaniment for Dance Techniques." *Dance Observer,* Vol. IV (February 1942).

Lockhart, Aileene. *Modern Dance: Building and Teaching Lessons.* Dubuque, Iowa: William C. Brown Company Publishers, 1957. Chapters XIX, XV, XVI.

Loxley, Ellis. "Waltzing Through Europe in the 19th Century." *Educational Dance,* Vol. II (October 1939), pp. 5-7.

McKinney, Howard D. and W. R. Anderson. *Discovering Music.* New York: American Book Co., 1952. Chapters 5, 7, 8, 12, 13, 14, 26.

Mains, Margaret S. *Modern Dance Manual.* Dubuque, Iowa: William C. Brown Company Publishers, 1950.

Mains, Margaret S. "Time Factors as Aids in Dance Composition." *Journal of Health, Physical Education and Recreation,* (March 1949), pp. 162-163+.

Mason, Bernard S. *Tom-Toms and Rattles.* New York: A. S. Barnes and Co., 1938.

Melcer, Fannie Helen. *Staging the Dance.* Dubuque, Iowa; William C. Brown Company Publishers, 1955. Chapter 7, "Accompaniment."

Mettler, Barbara. "What Is Rhythm?" *Educational Dance,* Vol. IV (March 1942), pp. 2-4.

Mettler, Barbara. "New Directions in Dance and Music." *Journal of Health, Physical Education and Recreation,* (February 1952), pp. 7, 34.

Murray, Ruth Lovell. *Dance in Elementary Education.* New York: Harper and Bros., 1953. Chapters VII, XXV.

Nettl, Paul. "Birth of the Waltz." *Dance Index,* (September 1946), pp. 207-227.

Nettl, Paul. *The Story of Dance Music.* New York: Philosophical Library, Inc., 1947.

Olive, Everett S. "A Closer Relationship Between Music and Dancing." *Educational Dance,* Vol. IV (February 1942), pp. 3-5.

O'Donnell, Mary P. "Dance Accompaniment for Children." *Journal of Health, Physical Education and Recreation,* (October 1946), pp. 469-470, 502-504.

O'Donnell, Mary P. and Sally Tobin Dietrich. *Notes for Modern Dance.* New York: A. S. Barnes and Co., 1938.

Oxford History of Music. Oxford: Clarendow Press, 1901-1905. Vol. I, II, III, IV, V, VI.

Page, Barbara. "Music for the Dance." *Theatre Arts,* Vol. 24 (September 1940), pp. 683-684.

Pease, Esther E. "Methods in Percussion." *Educational Dance,* Vol. III (November 1940), p. 10.

Phelps, Marie-Anne. "Chip on a Musician's Shoulder." *Dance Observer,* Vol. XIII (December 1946), pp. 121-122.

Phelps, Mary. "Poetry and Dance." *Dance Observer,* Vol. VIII (April 1941), pp. 52-53.

Porter, Evelyn. *Music Through Dance.* New York: Charles Scribner and Sons, 1938.

Pulver, J. "The Ancient Dance Forms." *Proceedings of Musical Association,* XXXIX.

Radir, Ruth. *Modern Dance for the Youth of America.* New York: A. S. Barnes and Co., 1944. Chapter VII.

Randolf, David. "A New Music Made With A Machine." *Horizon,* Vol. I, No. 3 (January 1959), pp. 50-55, 124-127.

Riegger, Wallingford. "Synthesizing Music and the Dance." *Dance Observer,* Vol. I (December 1934), pp. 84-85.

Roberts, Loma. "A Minimum Music Training for Teachers." *Dance Observer,* Vol. IV (March 1937), pp. 25, 28, 30.

Rudhyar, Dane. "The Companionate Marriage of Music and Dancing." *Dance Observer,* Vol. V (March 1938), pp. 37-38.

Russell, William. "Jazz Sources." *Dance Observer,* Vol. VII (December 1940), pp. 140-141, 144.

Sabin, Robert. "Music for the Dance." *Dance Observer,* Vol. VII (June-July 1940), pp. 82-83.

Sabin, Robert. "Gilding the Symphonies." *Dance Observer,* Vol. VII (January 1940), pp. 4, 10.

Sabin, Robert. "The Music of Mexico." *Dance Observer,* Vol. VII (June-July 1940), pp. 80-81.

Sabin, Robert. "The Sterility of Modern Music Criticism." *Dance Observer,* Vol. VIII (November 1941), pp. 118-119.

Sachs, Curt. *The Commonwealth of Art: Style in the Fine Arts, Music and the Dance.* New York: W. W. Norton and Co., Inc., 1946.

Sachs, Curt. *The History of Musical Instruments.* New York: W. W. Norton and Co., Inc., 1940.

Sachs, Curt. *Our Musical Heritage.* New York: Prentice Hall, Inc., 1955.

Seelye, Mary-Averett. "Words and Dance as an Integrated Medium." *Dance Observer,* Vol. IX (October 1942), pp. 104-105.

Sorell, Walter (editor). *The Dance Has Many Faces.* Cleveland: The World Publishing Co., 1951. "Music and the Dance." by Morton Gould, pp. 41-48.

Stearns, Marshall. *The Story of Jazz.* Oxford: Oxford University Press, 1958, Chapters 21, 22.

Todd, Arthur. "A New Union of Music and Dance." *Dance Observer,* Vol. XVIII (June-July 1951), pp. 84-85.

Tula. "Dancer-Accompanist-In-One." *Dance Observer,* Vol. XV (May 1958), pp. 53-54.

Waterman, Elizabeth. *The Rhythm Book.* New York: A. S. Barnes and Co., 1936.

White, Emily V. "Correlating Drama, Music and Dance." *Journal of Health, Physical Education and Recreation,* (September 1935), pp. 22-23+.

Wilker, Drusa. "Evaluation of Musical Composition for Modern Dance." *Educational Dance,* Vol. I (February 1938), pp. 3-4.

Chapter 14

DANCE ACCOMPANIMENT

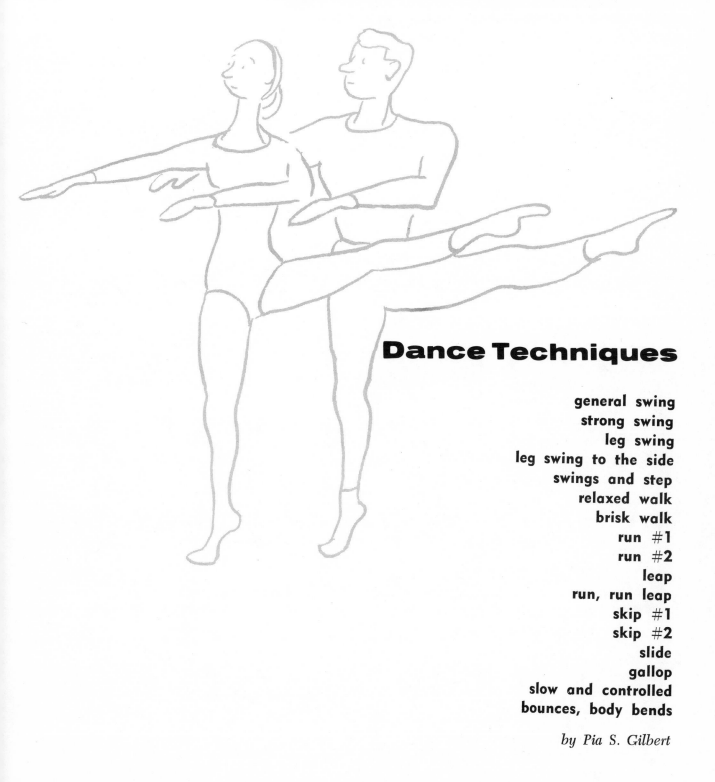

Dance Techniques

general swing
strong swing
leg swing
leg swing to the side
swings and step
relaxed walk
brisk walk
run #1
run #2
leap
run, run leap
skip #1
skip #2
slide
gallop
slow and controlled
bounces, body bends

by Pia S. Gilbert

General Swing

Strong Swing

Leg Swing

Leg Swing to the Side

Swing, Swing, Swing and Step

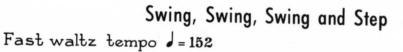

Relaxed, Bouncy Walk

Brisk Walk

Run

Run #2

80

81

Leaps

82

Run, Run, Leap

Skip #1 (light)

Skip #2: high—vigorous

Slide or Gallop

86

Gallop #2.

Fine

Da Capo al Fine

Slow and Controlled

Bounces and Body Bends

90

Dance Composition

accumulative rhythm
basso ostinato (ground bass)
two part form (A B)
ABA form
rondo

by Pia S. Gilbert

Accumulative Rhythm

Basso Ostinato (ground bass)

simile

sempre staccato

AB or Two Part Form

95

ABA Form

Rondo

Folk Dance Suite

waltz

schottische

mazurka

polka

hoedown

by Pia S. Gilbert

Little Waltz

104

Little Schottische

Mazurka

Vigorous ♩ = 104

Fine

107

Da Capo al Fine

Polka

Hoe-Down

110

Pre-classic Suite

pavane
gagliard
sarabande
allemande
courante

by Pia S. Gilbert

Pavane

Gagliard

Sarabande

Slow, heavy ♩ = 69

117

Courante

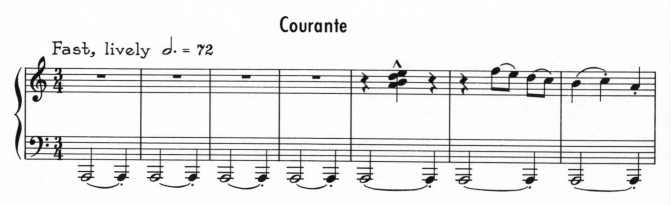

Allemande

Calligraphy: Wilhelmina Kerkhoven - Rotterdam.

120